SCIENCE AND RELIGION
IN AMERICAN THOUGHT

STANFORD UNIVERSITY PUBLICATIONS
UNIVERSITY SERIES
HISTORY, ECONOMICS, AND POLITICAL SCIENCE
VOLUME VIII

SCIENCE AND RELIGION
IN AMERICAN THOUGHT

The Impact of Naturalism

EDWARD A. WHITE

STANFORD UNIVERSITY PRESS, STANFORD, CALIFORNIA
LONDON: GEOFFREY CUMBERLEGE, OXFORD UNIVERSITY PRESS

1952

STANFORD UNIVERSITY PRESS
STANFORD, CALIFORNIA

LONDON: GEOFFREY CUMBERLEGE
OXFORD UNIVERSITY PRESS

———

THE BAKER AND TAYLOR COMPANY
HILLSIDE, NEW JERSEY

HENRY M. SNYDER & COMPANY
440 FOURTH AVENUE, NEW YORK 16

W. S. HALL & COMPANY
457 MADISON AVENUE, NEW YORK 22

———

Library of Congress Catalog Card Number: 52-5982

To my wife

Preface

THIS BOOK undertakes to analyze the positions of various American thinkers for whom the relationship of science and religion was a problem. It introduces the discussion with the work of John William Draper, a mid-nineteenth-century positivist, and continues with a consideration of representatives of the naturalist school from the impact of Darwinism in the work of John Fiske to the refinements of pragmatism or "instrumentalism" in the writings of John Dewey. It concludes with an appraisal of the controversy over the teaching of evolution in the public schools during the mid-1920's, when the issues were brought to popular attention.

The general question under examination is the relationship of science and religion as viewed by each thinker. What, for example, were the terms in which the problem was stated? Were science and religion held to be in harmony or in conflict? If in conflict, was there thought to be any possibility of reconciliation between them? If reconciliation was possible, how might it be achieved? The study also includes an estimate of the significance of each man for the discussion of the problem during the two generations in which naturalist presuppositions were dominant in American thought. Another study may carry the inquiry into a later period when naturalism was subject to a more critical analysis.

The viewpoint of this book is that of Christian thought and the positions examined are therefore appraised from the perspective of Christian presuppositions. The nature of the Christian interpretation is implicit rather than explicit in the critical sections of this study, and is not here under consideration. It may, however, not be inappropriate to suggest that the Christian interpretation implies, in the words of Reinhold Niebuhr, "a principle of meaning which transcends the world of meaning to be interpreted" as "the freedom of man's spirit transcends his rational faculties."

I wish to acknowledge my gratitude and indebtedness to Professor Matthew Evans of San Francisco State College for his constant encouragement, to Professor Emile Cailliet, Stuart Professor of Christian Philosophy in Princeton Theological Seminary, for his painstaking critical reading of the original manuscript and his suggestions for revision, to Miss Edith R. Mirrielees for helping to make the final chapter readable, to Professor Charles A. Allen, Editor of the Stanford University Press, for his indispensable guidance in matters affecting publication, and to my wife, Mary Jane White, for the kind of encouragement and support throughout that can never be fully discerned, much less acknowledged.

For permission to republish portions of this book previously published in *The Historian, The Pacific Spectator,* and *The Stanford Alumni Review* I wish to thank the editors of those journals.

EDWARD A. WHITE

STANFORD UNIVERSITY
January 1952

Contents

1

The Warfare of Science and Religion

IN 1925 Dr. David Starr Jordan, then Chancellor Emeritus of Stanford University, wrote a little book entitled *Science and Sciosophy*. "Sciosophy" was a new word coined by Jordan from the Greek *skia*, shadow, to denote "shadow of wisdom," or "organized ignorance."[1] "All of which," as the *San Francisco Examiner* put it, "translated into language that any well-read person can understand, makes it clear that the new . . . [word signifies] Applesauce! Banana Oil!"[2] In the book Dr. Jordan observed that "the history of science has been one long conflict with venerated ignorance, and in this conflict science has always won. Obstructions have been raised by men who thought the little they knew of the works and ways of the Creator was all that there was to be known. In spite of all impediment, science has forced the civilized world to acknowledge that . . . ignorance and superstition are perilous when used as guides for conduct, and that only the truth makes free."[3] In these words Dr. Jordan summarized the course of the relationship between science and religion in American thought for a generation. He was himself a document of the victory of science over religion which he described, having participated with his generation in its attempt to reconcile the conflict between them. When it was asked how science and religion could agree on the terms of reconciliation, one of Jordan's professors, William Herbert Carruth, replied, "Each in his own tongue," and illustrated his proposal in verse:

> A fire-mist and a planet,
> A crystal and a cell,
> A jellyfish and a saurian,
> And caves where the cave men dwell;
> Then a sense of law and beauty,
> And a face turned from the clod—
> Some call it Evolution,
> And others call it God.[4]

The indifference with which Jordan's generation viewed the claims of religion

---

[1] David Starr Jordan, *Science and Sciosophy* (*Betterhealthgrams*, Popular Series No. 2; San Francisco, January 1926), p. 3.

[2] *San Francisco Examiner*, July 31, 1925, p. 1.   [3] *Science and Sciosophy*, pp. 51, 53.

[4] William Herbert Carruth, *Each in His Own Tongue and Other Poems* (New York, 1909), p. 2.

testified to the triumph of the presuppositions of science. The legitimate object of human inquiry was indifferently God or evolution, which was the domain of science. All else was "sciosophy," "Banana Oil." Jordan's retirement in the late 1920's from active participation in the warfare of science marked almost precisely the close of a significant period in American thought. Thereafter there was less inclination to celebrate the nuptials of evolution and God.

John William Draper's *History of the Conflict of Religion and Science*, published in 1873, argued that science and religion were fundamentally in conflict because religion maintained its power through the institutionalized Church, whereas science sought to destroy the Church's pretensions to power by demonstrating the human origins of all religious institutions. He found the Church everywhere opposed to free scientific inquiry. Thus in the quest for truth the conflict between science and religion implied the opposition of reason and faith. Roman Catholicism claimed the supremacy of faith, science the supremacy of reason. Between these rival claims no compromise was possible: "Faith must render an account of herself to reason," for faith has been associated throughout history with fiction and fraud and organized impostures and delusions. Draper concluded that in the conflict of science and religion, Christianity, like Roman paganism, would disappear, leaving science alone in possession of the field because science "has given us grander views of the universe, more awful views of God."[5]

Jordan was a young instructor in biology, twenty-two years old, when Draper's book was published. A quarter-century later, when he had become president of Stanford, one of his brothers in the fraternity of university presidents, Andrew Dickson White of Cornell, availed himself of the research competencies of his professor of medieval history and produced his *History of the Warfare of Science with Theology in Christendom*, the work which more than any other kept the battle raging for the next generation.[6] Jordan was then forty-six. In 1923, when he was seventy-two, he still endorsed White's findings. "Have you ever read President White's 'Warfare of Science with Theology'?" he wrote to a correspondent. "You will find it very valuable in showing science from my point of view."[7] Between Draper and White, American thought had received the full impact of the Darwinian sociology. Hence White placed

---

[5] John William Draper, *History of the Conflict Between Religion and Science* (Introduction and Notes by Robert Arch; London, 1927), p. 270.

[6] Andrew Dickson White, *A History of the Warfare of Science with Theology in Christendom* (2 vols.; New York, 1897).

[7] David Starr Jordan to Scudder Klyce, December 26, 1923, Jordan Correspondence (MSS in the Stanford University Library, Stanford, Calif.), Vol. LXXXIII.

great emphasis upon evolution as a factor in the conflict. As he saw it, the conflict was between historical epochs, the modern world and the Middle Ages, not between social institutions, and he viewed the passage from the medieval to the modern epoch as accomplished within the processes of the evolutionary hypothesis. Thus the conflict between science and dogmatic theology was itself an instrument of progress, and the ultimate meaning of the doctrine of evolution was that it provided a basis for the eventual reconciliation of science and religion, for both were subject to the inexorable operation of its laws.

While Draper was fighting against the Church and White against vestigial medievalism, John Fiske, alternately Harvard professor and popular lecturer, happily set to work to demonstrate that the hostility of science and religion was apparent rather than real, and that a little right thinking would resolve it. From the publication of his *Outlines of Cosmic Philosophy* in 1874 through a succession of essays and addresses to the more specialized treatises at the turn of the century on the problems of God and immortality, Fiske attempted to assimilate fundamental Christian assumptions to the social Darwinism of his generation.[8]

Fiske held that under the harmonizing influence of the evolutionary process both science and religion worked toward the same ends. Indeed, much of the conflict between them had arisen, he thought, from an inadequate recognition of the fact that science and religion performed different functions in a common task, functions which, if properly conceived, involved no conflict whatever. "The business of science," Fiske maintained repeatedly, "is simply to ascertain in what manner phenomena coexist with each other or follow each other . . ."[9] If there appears to be a conflict, it arises from a failure to recognize that the advance guard of scientific knowledge is always involved in a struggle to maintain itself against the cruder science of yesterday.

Fiske's most significant contribution to the analysis of the relationship of science and religion, however, lay in the sensitivity to essential Christian concepts which even the crucible of social Darwinism could not completely reduce. He fully and explicitly embraced the Christian ideal, although he saw the hiatus between Christian possibilities and Christian pretensions, and he rightly struck at the presumption of Christian theologians in claiming perfect

[8] See John Fiske, *Outlines of Cosmic Philosophy, Based on the Doctrine of Evolution, with Criticisms on the Positive Philosophy* (2 vols.; Boston, 1874); *The Unseen World and Other Essays* (Boston, 1876); *Darwinism and Other Essays* (Boston, 1879); *The Idea of God as Affected by Modern Knowledge* (Boston, 1899); *Through Nature to God* (Boston, 1900).

[9] Fiske, "Darwinism Verified" (December 1876), in *Darwinism and Other Essays*, p. 7. See also *The Idea of God as Affected by Modern Knowledge*, pp. 101–2.

knowledge or complete truth. In a period characterized by the tendency of
the current idealism to make nature a product of mind, and of the popular
materialism to make mind a function of nature, it is worth noting that Fiske
preserved an area of independence and freedom for man by disassociating him
from the phenomena of nature with which he had to deal.[10]

At the turn of the century the reaction against the easy accommodation
of religious phenomena to the processes of natural science had begun. It was
most clearly voiced by William James, who saw that the current tendency to
refer science to external nature, rather than to mind, was responsible for much
of the confusion in the contemporary state of religion. For it followed that if
all truth inhered somehow in external nature, then the truths of religion must
also find their source and their validity in natural processes. Indeed, this was
the position at which the generation of Draper, White, and Fiske, who sought
in the doctrine of biological evolution the connection between science and religion, had arrived. But the easy accommodation of spiritual meaning to the
processes of evolution was fast losing its hold upon a growing circle of men,
among whom James counted himself. "I unhesitatingly repudiate the survival
theory of religion," he proclaimed in his Gifford lectures, "as being founded
on an egregious mistake."[11] How, then, to explain the popularity of the nature
religion in the later decades of the nineteenth century? James answered that
the nature religion permitted an indulgence of human ego which contradicted
the selflessness of the Christian ideal. This led to a religion of "healthy-
mindedness," proclaiming the natural goodness of man and denying the
existence of evil. Even the churches, said James, had for the past fifty years
substituted the religion of healthy-mindedness for Christianity. James rejected the nature religion as an inadequate explanation for man's religious
experiences and as a retreat from a profounder Christian metaphysics.[12]

Such a retreat from essential Christianity carried in James's opinion significant consequences for the relationship of science and religion for it undermined the ground of possible reconciliation. Both science and religion, he
held, depended for their meaning upon the assumption of the absolute validity of human personality. But whereas science generalizes from human

[10] "It is not merely that we refuse to attack Christianity because we recognize its necessary
adaptation to a certain stage of culture," Fiske wrote, "not yet passed by the average minds of the
community; it is that we still regard Christianity as, in the deepest sense, our own religion."
Outlines of Cosmic Philosophy, II, 502.

[11] William James, The Varieties of Religious Experience: A Study in Human Nature (New
York, 1902), p. 490. James proclaimed the bankruptcy of the natural religion in The Will to Believe: And Other Essays in Popular Philosophy (New York, 1908), p. 52.

[12] The Varieties of Religious Expereince, pp. 77 ff.

experience to arrive at cosmic abstractions, religion particularizes private and personal phenomena, to affirm concrete realities "in the completest sense of the term." Thus, "by being religious we establish ourselves in possession of ultimate reality at the very points at which reality is given us to guard."[13]

This is the argument that there is an area of experience into whose essential meaning science can never penetrate. To this argument, that a world which transcends nature does exist, and that it is the proper domain of religious experience, James brought as his strongest proof the evidence of tragedy and evil. The existence of tragedy continually emphasizes the need for a faith profound enough to transcend the crises of history, so that "where God is, tragedy is only provisional and partial, and shipwreck and dissolution are not the absolutely final things."[14] James's assertion of the transcendent reality of the individual religious experience offered a basis for the reconciliation of science and religion more profound than that of the social Darwinists. Their nexus was human personality itself, which comprehended alike the measurements of science and the evaluations of religion, but which signed no articles of capitulation with either.

As James became the leading philosophical spokesman for the scientific point of view, Jordan recognized his pre-eminence and invited him to Stanford. As late as 1921 he endorsed James's system as "an admirable exposition of our own notions and ideals."[15] In the decade of the 'twenties, however, he accepted the primacy of John Dewey as the interpreter of the philosophical presuppositions of science. Sensitive as always to a congenial doctrine, Jordan early proclaimed his "greater confidence in Dr. Dewey than in any other living philosopher." Dewey, Jordan asserted, "is a mental giant . . . that is his profession. My line is quite other, a simple fish-line."[16] Jordan counted on Dewey to uphold the claims of science against "sciosophy." How did he do it?

As Dewey clarified his position in the decade of the 'twenties, first in the Paul Carus lectures in 1925[17] and later in the Gifford lectures at Edinburgh,[18] it became apparent that he was departing more and more from the principles of William James. For whereas James had acknowledged the primacy of

---

[13] *Ibid.,* pp. 489, 491–92.

[14] *Ibid.,* p. 507.

[15] David Starr Jordan to Scudder Klyce, December 1, 1921, Jordan Correspondence, Vol. LXXXIII.

[16] Jordan to Scudder Klyce, October 6, 1919, and December 27, 1923, *ibid.,* Vol. LXXXIII.

[17] John Dewey, *Experience and Nature* (New York, 1925).

[18] John Dewey, *The Quest for Certainty: A Study of the Relation of Knowledge and Action* (New York, 1929).

religion in the realm of supernature and of science in the realm of nature, Dewey destroyed the distinction between the two realms. The modern mind, he believed, had accepted the conclusions of science but not its method, a contradiction which appeared as the conflict of science and religion. The central and "unscientific" proposition which kept the conflict alive was the claim of religion that facts and values were not equally amenable to the methods of science. Therefore, let us remedy the crisis, he said, by extending the philosophy of science into all the realms of human experience, especially where religious dogma has falsely separated the values men live by from the facts that constitute their lives.

From the standpoint of the supernaturalist, Dewey's position clarified the essential presuppositions of science, but it did not do justice to the claims of religion. In his Terry lectures in 1933,[19] Dewey limited the sphere of what he called "the religious" to its narrowest possible limits, namely, the unification of self for social action. But this view did not satisfy the soul that located the center of its being at a level from which even its own involvement in life became the object of its moral striving. The critics of Dewey's naturalism held that his answers were too simple to do justice to the most profound facts of human experience, notably those marked by personal tragedy or social catastrophe. It was clear that Dewey's solution to the conflict of science and religion destroyed the supernatural religion. If this was an outcome unacceptable to traditional religious thought, it was nevertheless thoroughly congenial to the conquest of "sciosophy" by science, and Dr. Jordan could pass his declining days in the gratifying knowledge that his early confidence had not been misplaced.

At the end of the period there was little agreement regarding the respective roles of science and religion in American life, although it was notable that the conflict had abated somewhat since the controversy over Darwinism in the age of Fiske and James. With Dewey the victory of naturalism over supernaturalism seemed complete. But even before the pretensions of industrialism were rudely shaken by the economic collapse of 1929, the assumption that the methods and axioms of science were absolute, and especially the claim that industrialism was good because science was true, was subject to searching scrutiny and criticism. It was now suggested, as by the critic John Crowe Ransom in *God Without Thunder* in 1930,[20] that the basic and underlying cause of the economic crisis particularly, as of the spiritual weakness of Amer-

---

[19] John Dewey, *A Common Faith* (New Haven, 1934).
[20] John Crowe Ransom, *God Without Thunder* (New York, 1930).

ica generally, was too much science. Science in Ransom's view was opposed
to religion as lust to love: science appropriated, conquered, exploited, and at
length destroyed Nature whereas religion respected, enjoyed, and worshiped
it. The secular religion which worshiped Christ as a man was clearly related
in Ransom's mind to the industrialization of modern life, which science had
created. This was a far cry from the current assertions of the apologists of
science, as, for example, of Henry Norris Russell, whose *Fate and Freedom*,
written as the Terry lectures at Yale in 1925, reaffirmed the religion of healthy-
mindedness. Immortality, Russell believed, was supported by God's wish to
give men more than they deserved or desired; the existence of God was
strengthened by the conviction that order and harmony must be real in a
truer sense than the strife and confusion which characterized the flux of
things.[21]

The conflict of the 'twenties was, in at least one respect, notable: it furnished the occasion for the first of the trenchant criticisms of modern society
by Reinhold Niebuhr, protestantism's outstanding theologian. The title of
Niebuhr's first book, published in 1927,[22] posited the question, *Does Civilization Need Religion?* In the course of his answer Niebuhr asserted that "The
plight of the West . . . [was] due to the complete bankruptcy of religious
forces and the unchallenged dominion of science . . . Applied science," he
predicted, "has created a civilization which may be as destructive of personality for the meagerly endowed multitudes as the natural poverty of Asia."[23]
Niebuhr charged that science threatened to annihilate human personality by
undermining the plausibility of the personalization of the universe, and by
creating a type of society in which human personality is easily debased. But
he denied that science had completely destroyed the comforting assurances of
religion, which, he said, "fails in its task if it does not save men from despair
as well as from undue pride and complacency."[24] The ultimate questions remained those of freedom and purpose, on the one hand, and justice, on the
other. Religion, Niebuhr held, is scientifically justified if freedom and purpose are found to have a place in the cosmic order. And if men are to mitigate
the cruelties which arise from the increased power that the conquest of nature
generates, they must rise to a higher level of insight and morality than naturalism implies.

[21] Henry Norris Russell, *Fate and Freedom* (New Haven, 1927), pp. 79, 167.
[22] Reinhold Niebuhr, *Does Civilization Need Religion? A Study in the Social Resources and
Limitations of Religion in Modern Life* (New York, 1927).
[23] *Ibid.,* p. 184.
[24] *Ibid.,* p. 218.

Thus the decade of the 'twenties closed with a vigorous challenge to the undisputed sway of scientific presuppositions in American thought. It is the thesis of this book that a generation of conflict between science and religion had issued in a clarification of the place of religion in American life and introduced a notable revival of religious thought. Whether the quality of contemporary religious thought is adequate to the current crisis is a question of the hour.

2

The Positive Science
John William Draper

IN THE FOLLOWING discussion of the relationship of science and religion in American thought in the late nineteenth and early twentieth centuries, no arbitrary point of beginning can be selected. Nevertheless, the decade of the 1860's seems crucial for precipitating the conflict between religion and science as it developed during the next three generations. This study begins with an examination of the writings of John William Draper, for whose publications the decade of the 1860's is central. Draper was a transitional figure who undertook to formulate the doctrines of positivistic science and to apply them to the study of history at just the period when social and religious thought was receiving the full impact of the new developmental biology. Darwin's *Origin of Species* was published in 1859. In 1860 Draper read a paper at the meeting of the British Association for the Advancement of Science at Oxford in which he drew an analogy between man and society and proposed that society should be studied in terms of physiological principles. At the same meeting there occurred the famous debate between Samuel Wilberforce, Bishop of Oxford, and Thomas Huxley, in which Wilberforce attacked, and Huxley defended, the Darwinian doctrine. Thus, in immediate juxtaposition the society of British scholars met the old and the new. Draper's positivism tackled the problem of the relationship of science and religion but soon gave way to Huxley's evolutionism, and in America the new doctrine carried the field. The period covered in this study begins with the formulation of a new issue in the warfare of science and religion. Whereas Draper was chiefly concerned with the analytical sciences and their relevance to human problems—that is to say, with what chemistry and physics and especially physiology and medicine could tell about man's nature and life—such of his successors as John Fiske and Andrew D. White undertook to relate the findings of the biological sciences, and particularly the doctrine of evolution, to human history and human sociology.

The decade of the 1860's witnessed other crucial developments in the Western world which were not unrelated to the conflict of science and religion. The English sociologist Benjamin Kidd, writing shortly after the out-

break of the first World War, described what seemed to him a notable feature
of the preceding fifty years:

There is a striking feature which we may perceive to be characteristic of the half-
century which preceded the war which began in 1914. At the centre of every movement of opinion in the West the same fact is to be noticed. There is visible a gradual
falling back upon first principles, a retreat all along the line to those conditions of
elemental force under which the civilization of the West first came into being.[1]

Kidd's arithmetic was accurate to the point of the prodigious. Take fifty from
1914 and you find Bismarck beginning the wars of German unification with
the conquest of Denmark, Grant and Sherman about to administer the coup
de grâce to the faltering Confederacy, and Pope Pius IX denouncing in the
Syllabus of Errors the threats of nationalism and liberalism to the dominant
position of the Church. The American Civil War, perhaps more than any
other event of the decade, emphasized the triumph of industrial organization
and the power which accrued to its masters. If one is to judge by the books
which came from his pen during these years, Draper was quick to appreciate
the importance of these developments. In 1867 he published his analysis of
post-Civil War problems under the title *Thoughts on the Future Civil Policy
of America*, followed in the period 1867–70 by his three volume *History of the
American Civil War*. The principles of his *Human Physiology*, which appeared in 1856, he applied to the *History of the Intellectual Development of
Europe* in 1861. These works were both informed by the principles of positivism, the one in a strictly scientific field, the other in the field of the social
studies. But the elements of force inherent in the earlier papal pronouncement were so clearly emphasized by the decree of papal infallibility, affirmed
by the Vatican Council which met at the summons of Pope Pius in 1870, that
Draper responded in 1873 with the work for which he is best known, his
History of the Conflict Between Religion and Science.

By virtue of his family background, John William Draper came naturally
to an interest in religion, and because of his professional education and career,
he occupied a position of leadership in mid-nineteenth-century science in
America. Draper was born in England and came to Virginia with his mother
and sister after his father's death. His father had been a Roman Catholic, but
had come under the influence of John Wesley who converted him to Method-
ism during one of Wesley's revivalistic expeditions in England. Draper's wife
had also been a Roman Catholic, but after her marriage she turned to liberal

[1] Benjamin Kidd, *The Science of Power* (New York, 1918), p. 9.

Anglicanism, although Draper himself did not maintain any formal connection with an ecclesiastical group. Nevertheless, he continued on terms of friendly intimacy with many liberal clergymen and expressed religious views which have been described as resembling those "of an eighteenth-century Deist who sensed divinity in the general order of the universe."[2]

Draper's professional life was spent as a teacher of chemistry and medicine at New York University, and as the organizer and administrative head of the medical school which was established at the University. Medical research, however, was always too narrow to contain him. Attracted to the field of intellectual history, he did his most substantial work in arguing the relevance of such positivistic principles as the determining influence of climate upon the history of European civilization and upon the conflict of sections in America. In his *History of the Intellectual Development of Europe* Draper attempted to do for the whole of Europe what Buckle had done for England alone. Throughout his work he emphasized the significance of science for the growth of civilization, and in his *History of the Conflict Between Religion and Science* he identified as the antagonist of science the institutionalized church with its pretensions to absolute power. In the gradual victory of science over religion, Draper gave great credit to the stimulus which successive invasions from Africa into Europe, culminating with the Saracenic influx of the eighth century, had provided for the intellectual awakening of Europe. Draper's interest in science led him to explore extensively the contributions of Saracenic scholars and made him one of the earliest to evaluate their influence upon the development of Western civilization.

Draper's *Human Physiology* gave more than incidental attention to religious questions, particularly in Book II of the work, which Draper called "Dynamical Physiology" in contradistinction to the "Statical Physiology" of Book I, in which he considered the "conditions" of life as distinguished from its "course." In the concluding chapters of the second book, he discussed the influence of physical factors on the progress of civilization and gave an account of the history of Western society. He stated in the Preface that he proposed to take every opportunity to explain man's moral nature because he believed that "the right progress of society depends on its religious opinions."[3] Although a positivist, Draper was no materialist. He believed in the existence and immortality of the soul, and he was confident that positive

[2] Ellwood Hendrick, "John William Draper," *Dictionary of American Biography,* V (Allen Johnson and Dumas Malone, eds.; New York, 1930), 441.

[3] John William Draper, *Human Physiology, Statical and Dynamical; or, The Conditions and Course of the Life of Man* (New York, 1856), p. v.

science would "inevitably conduct us to the truth" about them.[4] This truth, would vindicate rather than repudiate essential religious notions. It would validate the methods of science and show that what was vital in our religious tradition was more nearly akin to the active and practical civilization of the West than to the otherworldliness and resignation of the East.

Historically considered, the conflict of science and religion was precipitated, Draper held, by the Saracenic invasion of Europe in the eighth century. This, however, was no new phenomenon in the history of Europe. Twice before, impulses from Egypt had carried new peoples into Europe, once under the Pharaohs and again under the Ptolemies, and each time the hesitant civilization of the West had taken on new vigor from the contact with peoples from a warmer climate:

the old white inhabitants of Europe [Draper observed] were not able to commence their civilization from their own interior resources, but were thrown into that career by the example and aid of a more southern and darker people, whose climate was more favorable. The artificial change which spread by degrees over Europe, through the introduction of more comfortable modes of life, at last compensated for the natural climate defect, and the European entered on the course of advancement, undergoing . . . a physical as well as a mental change.[5]

Until the Saracenic invasions, Christianity had been a religion of the cloister and the chancel; and the Koran of the Arabians did not, even after the establishment of Moslem supremacy in Spain, constitute a real challenge to the Bible. But with the physical science of the Saracens it was quite a different story. Its spread, Draper held, was the true foundation of modern national power, for it promoted the development of material resources and the introduction of useful inventions. The Saracens, according to Draper, moved the intellectual center of Europe from Rome to Cordova, thereby destroying the supremacy of the Mediterranean area and eventually turning the face of Europe to the West. But most of all, the manner of scientific thought challenged the authoritarianism of the early Church, and thereby produced the controversy between science and religion which has characterized modern times.[6]

The significance of Draper's *Human Physiology* in the history of the conflict of religion and science lies in its illustration of the claim that mid-nineteenth-century positivism could resolve the conflict and provide an adequate intellectual and moral basis for life in the contemporary world. Draper believed that the current schools of metaphysical philosophy were unpromising

[4] *Human Physiology, Statical and Dynamical*, pp. v–vi.
[5] *Ibid.*, p. 634.
[6] *Ibid.*, p. 635.

for the solution of this problem because their empiricism was untested by the methods of science, and that, therefore, a new system must be devised. A system based upon the presuppositions of physical science, he thought, had a good prospect of success. Since "God has framed our understanding to grasp all these things," Draper argued, man may be assured of his power to comprehend all the conditions of his life.[7] Among these conditions, Draper would assign first place to that principle which animates man's physiological system, a principle both self-conscious and immortal, called the soul. The treatment of this principle lay properly within the province of physiology, but circumstances had yielded its custody to the psychologist or to the theologian. Yet the physiologist, and especially the practitioner of medicine, whose science promised to rival in future times the precision of mechanical engineering, must take every opportunity "to assert and to uphold the doctrine of the oneness, the immortality, the accountability of the soul," and to do so with "whatever evidence the structure of the body can furnish."[8] Draper was confident that thereby the great truths of religion would be brought "into the region of physical demonstration . . ."[9]

It was characteristic of the physical scientist to maintain that moral doctrines depended for their validity, not merely upon observed human behavior, as the empiricist held, but upon immutable law stamped by the Creator upon the essential organization and structure of the universe. Thus the universe required the existence of the soul to animate the cerebral structure, which without the soul would remain absolutely inert, in the same way that it required the external agencies of light and sound to activate the mechanisms for sight and hearing.[10] And not only the existence of the soul but its immortality as well was to be considered "one of the organic dogmas of our race,"[11] because it was stamped so firmly upon the human mind, Draper thought, that not even education and training could adequately destroy it. Such conceptions were supported physiologically, he believed, by the mechanism of "inverse vision," an instrument which enabled man to hold before his inner eye in all their vividness the motivating moral and spiritual ideals. Thus the idea of immortality was held by communities of men in isolation from their fellows and without either revelation or intellectual power adequate to reach this proposition by reason.

Can there be [Draper asked], in a philosophical view, anything more interesting than the manner in which these defects have been provided for, by implanting in

---

[7] *Ibid.*, p. 25. [8] *Ibid.*, p. 24. [9] *Ibid.*, p. 26.
[10] *Ibid.*, p. 285. [11] *Ibid.*, p. 548.

the very organization of every man the means of constantly admonishing him of these facts, of recalling them with an unexpected vividness before him, even after they have become so faint as almost to die out?[12]

This mechanism performed the functions which we attribute to conscience or insight, preserving for us "the most solemn facts with which we can be concerned," and exhibiting them most vividly in moments of repose or of sickness, when the influence of external things is diminished.[13] The stamp upon our cerebral organization, according to Draper, is responsible for our ideas of what is good and evil, of virtue, of the efficacy of penance and of prayer, of rewards and punishments, and of another world.[14] It decrees that women are essentially religious and apply their faith to almost all the ordinary affairs of life.[15] It favors an anthropomorphic rather than a pantheistic notion of deity because the former "specializes and intensifies our ideas . . . embodies our recollections, and restores to us our dead."[16] And it responds to our form of social organization, as when it finds the notion of God as universal Father and Giver of all good more acceptable than the conception of the Deity as the Almighty Maker of the world.[17]

The idea of immortality, Draper held, was indeed a part of man's essential nature; but it need not be accepted merely on faith, for the methods of science demonstrated it to be true and thus removed one of the great causes of possible conflict with religion. One of the stumbling blocks to the reconciliation of science and religion had long been the reluctance of science to speak to the issue of man's immortality, which religion always steadfastly maintained. Positive science could now bring support to this essential doctrine. For did not science assume the existence of the external world, even to the extent of predicting its future state, so far as astronomical calculations were concerned, a thousand years hence? The question of immortality, he believed, presented no more difficult problem. If we can assert the existence of an external world, we can with equal assurance claim the existence of an "external" life. "We have precisely the same reason for believing the existence of the immortal spirit," Draper held, "that we have for knowing that there is an external world. The two facts are of the same order."[18] Perhaps, indeed,

---

[12] *Human Physiology, Statical and Dynamical,* p. 415.
[13] *Ibid.,* p. 416.
[14] *Ibid.,* p. 544.
[15] *Ibid.,* p. 546. But Draper notes that, nevertheless, "when she finds that she has been deceived she is ever distrustful."
[16] *Ibid.,* pp. 286–87.
[17] *Ibid.,* p. 548.
[18] *Ibid.,* p. 550.

this argument was by analogy, but the case need not rest on analogy alone.

The nineteenth-century materialist commonly assumed the indestructibility of matter and energy, and this Draper took as additional support for immortality, in that it implied the indestructibility of conscious identity. It was consistent with the findings of science about the external world to expect modification or change in the state of the soul but not loss of existence.[19] Although no Darwinian, Draper was sensitive to the fact of change, both in the physical world and in society. "The whole course of life," he stated, "from its very beginning, has been one of development and concentration."[20] An examination of the history of human development made it clear, he thought, that controlling law and unfolding purpose pointed to "the isolation of a conscious intelligence" as the objective of the entire process. Therefore, if the process of development which science had revealed in the past was extended into the future, one must conclude that the end of the process would achieve the complete realization of human consciousness, in circumstances which were not affected by the mortality of its present physical appurtenances. And what more natural conclusion in view of the history of the human organism from conception to death? Draper asked. Without loss or injury the human spirit had used and abandoned, one after another, a succession of mechanisms, each adequate to the present need, each put aside when it had finished its duty. The evidence of embryology, for example, showed how many different systems of respiration and of nutrition had provided oxygen and food prior to birth, and physiology indicated how complete were the transformations through which the bodily organs passed in the course of life. Yet the human spirit was not only unaffected by these changes but grew in strength and integrity through them all. For these reasons, Draper concluded that the impression of immortality was not based upon instinct alone:

after surviving so many mutations [he insisted], the removal of so many of what seemed to be its firm and essential supports, we are justified in expecting that it will bear without ruin the entire withdrawal of the whole scaffolding.[21]

So if the conflict between science and religion rested on any disagreement about the future state of the soul, Draper was confident that he had resolved it.

If the conflict of science and religion was peculiarly a Western problem, precipitated by the impact of Saracenic science upon a society dominated by

19 *Ibid.*, p. 549.
20 *Ibid.*, p. 551.
21 *Ibid.*, p. 550.

the Church, one would expect to see repercussions of the conflict on the character of Western man. Draper believed that human character was capable of improvement in proportion to man's ability to escape the domination of the Church, on the one hand, and to apply the teachings of science, on the other. The Reformation, he held, vindicated the human right of private judgment, an advantage immeasurably greater than any attendant inconvenience from the multiplication of sects.[22] He maintained that science had made the European the moral superior of the Asiatic, in spite of a common and natural depravity of the human heart which had led in the East to concubinage and in the West to polygamy and prostitution.[23] Western man, he said, demanded a reason for the course of life and its circumstances, refused to accept the tyranny either of nature or of society, and accepted the consequences of his revolt against them.[24] His noblest attribute was his universal charity,[25] and his most essential quality of mind his capacity for analysis. From the one flowed his exertions to diffuse the blessings conferred on him by Providence upon other peoples; from the other, his propensity to divide his religious life into numberless denominations.[26] Western man's power of analysis, Draper believed, carried with it also the capacity for progress, an ability to apply his knowledge to practical needs, which marked off the European from the Asiatic.

It is this which pre-eminently distinguishes the European [Draper observed]; that whatever scientific discovery he makes, or whatever invention occurs to him, he forthwith applies it to economic advantage, and is thereby perpetually impressing a change on his own state.[27]

And yet, despite Draper's belief that science had given Western man the control of his life and his environment, he could not adequately solve the dilemma of the extent of man's freedom within the system of natural law. The best he could do was to assert a kind of racial determinism, within which man's freedom was but illusory, and to the achievement of whose ends all of man's actions were blindly dedicated:

The acts of man, though they may have the aspect of free-will as regards himself, are automatic as regards the race. He is employed in achieving a result of which he is utterly ignorant; he is concerned in a work of the effects of which he is un-

22 *Human Physiology, Statical and Dynamical*, p. 625.
23 *Ibid.*, p. 594.
24 *Ibid.*, p. 593.
25 *Ibid.*
26 *Ibid.*, p. 637.
27 *Ibid.*

conscious. He is like a bee, which doubtless experiences a certain pleasure in flying from flower to flower, the gratification of an obscure desire in constructing cell after cell, its individual delight ministering to a public good of the nature of which it is wholly unconscious.[28]

But if Draper did not succeed in making a plausible connection between human freedom and human destiny, it is worth remembering that he saw the problem and that he did not pretend to solve it by denying the reality of either horn of the dilemma. He believed that human action was significant and that its ultimate end was the perfect freedom of the immortal human spirit.

Just as human actions were made meaningful by their fulfillment of a higher law, so also, Draper believed, social development illustrated certain great principles which promised to mitigate the differences among nations and races. He held that, however great the differences between European and Asiatic, both recognized common principles of religion and justice.[29] He considered Mohammedanism as an instrument for bringing the peoples of Africa out of barbarism to a knowledge of Western morality and religion.[30] These developments were but the supreme application of that essential aspect of man's nature which instinctively grasped moral principles and affirmed the existence of the soul and its immortality. The human mind, whether individual or collective, moves in a recognized direction toward the discernment of absolute principles which are valid for all peoples in all ages. We cannot improve upon the Ten Commandments, said Draper, for their essential proscriptions appeal to the understanding of intelligent men of all nations.[31] Thus there emerge in human history, as in anthropology, types to which we refer for our judgment of the acts of individuals. These types represent races or nations. They are to be identified, Draper held, by the representative quality of their mental progress, their manner of thinking and of acting. At a higher level of universality one may discover a more fundamental type still.[32] Thus Draper was willing to go the whole distance in his application of physiological principles to human morality and human history. If, indeed, the proper study of mankind was man, it could be expected to reveal the principles of morality and the laws of history with an exactitude equal to the postulates of physiology and medicine.

The application of these physiological principles to man in his social relationships was the problem of Draper's second book, first published in 1861

[28] *Ibid.*, p. 622.   [29] *Ibid.*, pp. 601–2.
[30] *Ibid.*, p. 597.
[31] *Ibid.*, p. 602.
[32] *Ibid.*, p. 611.

in two volumes, his *History of the Intellectual Development of Europe.* In this work Draper undertook to supply the historical evidence for the thesis which he had presented in his paper at Oxford in 1860 before the British Association for the Advancement of Science. The main thesis of the book is that the physiological development of man as an individual establishes the laws which control the growth of society, that, as Draper put it, "man is the archetype of society. Individual development is the model of social progress."[33]

Draper devoted about two-thirds of the book to a consideration of European intellectual history. In the remainder he gave extended attention to the history of Greece, with introductory chapters on law in nature and the topography and ethnography of Europe, and digressions on the development of Hindu and Egyptian civilization, Roman civilization, and Saracenic civilization. In describing the history of civilization, Draper applied the five ages of man as an individual to his history as a member of society. Thus he divided the history of Western Europe as of Greece into the Age of Credulity, the Age of Inquiry, the Age of Faith, the Age of Reason, and the Age of Decrepitude.[34] Europe, according to Draper, was still in the Age of Reason, which she had entered in the sixteenth century after careful preparation by contacts with the Saracens and the rise of criticism. The great aim of nature, he maintained, was intellectual improvement, a fact which was equally clear whether the investigator turned his attention to the individual or to the nation. Just as human development proceeded from automatism, through instinct, to intelligence, so also the end of the historical studies was properly the description of the progress of the intellectual life of society.

In man himself [Draper wrote] the three distinct modes of life occur in an epochal order through childhood to the most perfect state. And this holding good for the individual, since it is physiologically impossible to separate him from the race, what holds good for the one must also hold good for the other.[35]

In this fashion he proposed to bridge the gap between the individual and society.

The prime assumption from which Draper as physical scientist and positivist approached the study of society was that natural law controlled social development. "Social advancement," he wrote, "is as completely under the control of natural law as is bodily growth."[36] Proofs of the dominion of

[33] John William Draper, *History of the Intellectual Development of Europe* (rev. ed.; New York, 1876), I, 2.
[34] *Ibid.*, I, 19.
[35] *Ibid.*, II, 394–95.
[36] *Ibid.*, I, iii.

law were to be found, he believed, in the study of man's physiological development, in the relationship of animal forms in the midst of which he lives, and in the orderly succession of animal life which has emerged in time.[37] The triumph of the conception of law has gradually displaced superstition. This has been the achievement of science, he argued, and its consequence for religion was the formulation of a nobler conception of deity, "one Almighty Being, who rules the universe according to reason and therefore according to law."[38] Draper's vision of a universe governed by a rational, law-abiding, and single deity was a conception natural to a mid-nineteenth-century physical scientist. A period of great social upheaval sought refuge in the dominion of law, to which the physical scientist contributed by his deification of the principles of order and regularity. If, too often, the reign of law was not adequately distinguished from the rule of force, that lay outside the inquiry of the scientist. For Draper it was enough to describe the advantages of law over caprice, of an eternal Providence over the evanescent affairs of mere men:

Such a conception commends itself to the intellect of man by its majestic grandeur. It makes him discern the eternal in the vanishing of present events and through the shadows of time. From the life, the pleasures, the sufferings of humanity, it points to the impassive; from our wishes, wants, and woes, to the inexorable. Leaving the individual beneath the eye of Providence, it shows society under the finger of law. And the laws of Nature never vary; in their application they never hesitate or are wanting.[39]

The conception of an inexorable law is meaningful as an anchor against chaos. But even an anchor must bite firmly into the ocean floor if it is to hold the ship steady in the gale. But for Draper, who adhered to a belief in the control of "laws as unchangeable as destiny,"[40] there was no escape from the dominion of law and, therefore, no release from its tyranny. The present universe, for example, Draper believed to have had a beginning and to have an end, but he held that it was but one of a multiplicity of such universes which would be repeated infinitely in the future as they had existed endlessly in the past. Therefore,

that which is contemporary with us is only an example of the countless combinations of a like kind, which in ancient times have one after another vanished away.[41]

One may well ask whether in such a conception of law all individuality may

[37] Ibid., II, 394.   [38] Ibid., I, 4.
[39] Ibid., I, 20.
[40] Ibid., II, 336.
[41] Ibid.

not be lost, and the meaning of history, which is essentially particular and unique, lapse into insignificance.

But if inexorability was, as Draper saw it, the essential quality of law in nature and in history, it remains to inquire what the law was that was so inexorable in its incidence and unchangeable in its operation. From his studies of society in its historical development Draper was prepared to answer. He observed that man in America had advanced in the course of his civilization along the same lines as man in Europe and in Asia, devising the same institutions, acknowledging the same intentions, and responding to the same desires. Similar results, he recognized, implied a similar cause.

What, then [he asked], is there possessed in common by the Chinese, the Hindoo, the Egyptian, the European, the American: Surely not the climate, nor equal necessities, nor equal opportunity. Simply nothing but this—corporeal organization! As automatons constructed in the same way will do the same things, so, in organic forms, sameness of structure will give rise to identity of function and similarity of acts. The same common sense guides men all over the world.[42]

This, then, was the essential law guiding history as it determined human growth: Stamped upon the minds of men by their essential nature were qualities which governed their development. Oppose these inherent tendencies and society will disintegrate; cherish and nurture them and reap the rewards of progressive improvement. Science yielded these eternal truths about the nature of man. These truths religion must recognize and incorporate in its teachings or the warfare between science and religion will be incessant and total. Much of Draper's *Intellectual History* was devoted to an illustration of these propositions.

The victory of science in its conflict with religion in the West, according to Draper, had changed the attitude of the European toward the nature of the world and of man and had given to the West a point of view markedly different from that of the countries of Asia. To the Oriental mind the world is merely a gigantic engine which runs through a predestined series of operations. But to the European the world is the creation of a personal God, "who considers and orders events in a vast panorama before him."[43] It followed that the element of personality, most characteristic of the Western concept of deity, should also distinguish the Western concept of man. Human life could not be symbolized by the flame of a lamp, an impermanent and transitory aspect of matter which lost its identity when the flame was extinguished. Instead,

---

[42] *History of the Intellectual Development of Europe*, II, 187.
[43] *Ibid.*, II, 365.

the European believed in "an individualized impersonation of the soul, and an expectation of its life hereafter." The body was held to be but the instrument through which "that mysterious principle," the human spirit, worked its designs in the world. In spite of his endorsement of the principle of natural law, Draper held clearly that the victory of science had supported, rather than endangered, the integrity of human personality.

Not only the contrast between East and West but also the conflict of science and religion through the ages was clear evidence to Draper that the victory of science meant liberty while the control of religion threatened social stagnation. Patristic learning, for example, had generated nothing except "hundreds of . . . folios filled with obsolete speculation, oppressing the shelves of antique libraries, enveloped in dust, and awaiting the worm."[44] On the other hand, when the first stirrings of science in the sixteenth century precipitated the conflict with religion, the Church, according to Draper, was soon forced to grant an armed truce which permitted free thought for science in return for "an unmolested state" for theology.[45] Another great step forward, he felt, was the separation of Church and State achieved by the American Revolution. For whereas religious unity implies tyranny, the multiplication of sects gives the greatest possible opportunity for liberty.

In this respect unity and liberty are in opposition; as the one diminishes, the other increases. The Reformation broke down unity; it gave liberty to masses of men grouped together in sufficient numbers to insure their position; it is now invisibly, but irresistibly making steps, never to be stayed until there is an absolute mental emancipation for man.[46]

He therefore pointed to America as the nation in which the Reformation had advanced farthest, because it had achieved the widest diversity of religious affiliation and practice. But in America, he felt, the disintegration of religious unity had not weakened religion; on the contrary, it had refreshed it and restored it to popular service. By voluntary contributions, rather than by compulsory levies, America had built churches, sustained the clergy, and undertaken enterprises of piety, education, and mercy. As a result the ministry had won new respect and had achieved a position of leadership long since lost in countries still dominated by a single church. Thus the history of Western civilization proved, Draper thought, that religious life was most vigorous where the analytical capacities of science enjoyed highest repute.

44 *Ibid.*, I, 387.
45 *Ibid.*, II, 150.
46 *Ibid.*, II, 227.

To what conclusions, then, did Draper's analysis of the intellectual history of Europe lead him? Granting that society, like individuals, developed according to law and achieved its fullest stature when it did not hinder man's natural instinct for liberty—what could be expected of the future? For one thing, Draper professed a strong belief in the doctrine of progress:

the conclusion inculated by these doctrines . . . is that all political institutions—imperceptibly or visibly, spontaneously or purposely—should tend to the improvement and organization of national intellect.[47]

But such an improvement of the national mind was not without serious consequences for man's attitude toward himself and the world. It was clear to Draper that the conflict had vindicated scientific truth against all efforts to modify or control it. The persecution of science had failed utterly to accomplish its suppression.

In vain was Bruno burnt and Galileo imprisoned; the truth forced its way, in spite of all opposition, at last. The end of the conflict was a total rejection of authority and tradition, and the adoption of scientific truth.[48]

Few would disagree that the protection of free inquiry against coercion from whatever source was a gain for the rights of human personality. The conflict had achieved freedom *from* authority and tradition, Draper argued, but freedom *for* what? Was it possible that the gain in liberty was perhaps accompanied by a loss in direction? Draper did not offer any real consideration of this issue, although he recognized that when the Church gave over its control of intellectual inquiry, it also lost its direction of human purposes. The universe was no longer qualified at every point, as the schoolmen had taught, by questions of relevance and destiny:

what has become [Draper asked] of the time-honoured doctrine of the human destiny of the universe? that doctrine for the sake of which the controversy I have described . . . was raised.[49]

What, indeed, had become of this doctrine? In the first emancipation of modern science from ecclesiastical control the sense of power which accompanies any new freedom momentarily obscured the loss of purpose. Truth for truth's sake, rather than science for society, served to describe the attitude of the modern world toward the place of intellectual inquiry in the scheme of human activities. The view that all truth was affected by a religious interest

---

[47] *History of the Intellectual Development of Europe*, II, 395.
[48] *Ibid.*, II, 293.
[49] *Ibid.*

which touched every investigator with responsibility for the uses to which his discovery was put had not survived the liberation of science. Instead of a "human destiny," that is, a fulfillment consistent with human purposes, the positive scientist held that the universe had merely a "natural destiny," that is, no fulfillment at all, only an inexorable obedience to natural law. Such a de-humanization of the universe was a consequence of the characteristic attitudes of Western science as Draper saw them, attitudes which emphasized analysis to the detriment of any integrated and systematic view of human life in its total context of nature and history.

While he was writing *The Intellectual Development of Europe*, Draper became convinced that the principles which explained European history ap-plied with equal force to America. In the winter of 1864, when he was invited to deliver a course of four lectures before the New York Historical Society, he undertook to develop the familiar thesis that natural law governed the de-velopment of the United States. These lectures in expanded form were pub-lished in 1867 under the title *Thoughts on the Future Civil Policy of America*.

The work of the historian, Draper held, was to predict the inevitable course through which a nation must pass. This he could do if he recognized that "the government of the world is accomplished by immutable law."[50] Draper devoted the first chapter of his book to the influence of climate. He concluded that although climate imposed unalterable limits upon the develop-ment of animal forms and social institutions, man could modify its effects by personal locomotion. The ease of movement of the American people, he said, was responsible for the variety and stability of American institutions, where-fore he concluded that legislation to sustain and encourage it was necessary to ensure national progress.[51] Natural law, however, was not alone responsible for America's characteristic development and her promise of greatness. Draper recognized social forces as powerful influences upon national character and history. In the case of the United States, the most important of these factors was emigration, which had peopled the Atlantic seaboard and by mid-century was making the northern Ohio Valley the granary of Europe.[52] In remarking the significance of the Westward movement, both for its conquest of unoc-cupied lands and for the resulting deterioration of social and intellectual stand-ards, Draper anticipated the later frontier historians. He noticed that by and large the movement of population was along parallels of latitude into similar

[50] John William Draper, *Thoughts on the Future Civil Policy of America* (New York, 1867), pp. iv, 34.
[51] *Ibid.*, p. 86.
[52] *Ibid.*, p. 166.

climate zones, thus reproducing conditions and social forms immediately to the East, but he predicted that future lines of movement would bring native population into the South and Asiatic immigrants into the Pacific states, thus altering markedly the prevailing patterns of society.[53]

What was most remarkable, however, about Draper's analysis of American civil policy was his departure from the natural determinism characteristic of the scientific positivist. Although he wrote much about the controlling influence of natural forces, he devoted the final chapters of his book to emphasizing the power of ideas in history. Ideas, Draper held, are really more powerful than natural conditions. The power of ideas was well illustrated, he thought, by the expansive force of Islam and by the resistance of the Jews. Islamic dedication to the oneness of Allah and the prophecy of Mohammed had carried the Saracens west to Spain and east to Singapore, while Jewish faith in the coming of the Messiah and in the exclusiveness of Old Testament truth had preserved the Hebrew nation against the ravages of conquest and of time.[54]

Such is the progress [he concluded], and such, often, the power of an Idea. From the mind in which it first originated it may spread, until at last, physically and intellectually, whole continents may be involved. It is useless, then, to say that ideas have no force. In truth, they govern the world.[55]

The course of modern civilization, according to Draper, could be understood only by discovering the essential idea in terms of which it was developing.

The power of ideas in the history of the Arabian and the Jewish peoples served to illustrate on a smaller scale, he thought, the larger pattern of historical development. Just as monotheism and the Messianic prophecy had held the Saracens and the Hebrews together, so also the modern world could achieve unity and power only through its own central theme. This "grander idea," under which modern civilization was moving, was not the dominance of natural law but rather the contrary assumption, that natural forces could themselves be controlled and physical obstacles to human progress be overcome. Thus, at the end, it was in human freedom rather than in natural order that he placed his strongest hope and faith for the future of civilization.[56]

Draper was well aware, however, that the mere power of ideas did not guarantee their victory over the forces ranged against them without vigilance and struggle. That was why, he argued, the history of civilization could be written in terms of the conflict of science and religion, for science always

---

[50] *Thoughts on the Future Civil Policy of America*, p. 170.   [54] *Ibid.*, p. 210.
[55] *Ibid.*, p. 197.   [56] *Ibid.*, p. 211.

supported the power of ideas, whereas religion all too frequently supported particular organized groups instead. He regretted that it was no longer possible to discuss the meaning of Biblical literature according to the rules of literary criticism because partisans in the controversy had appropriated and affirmed the very propositions whose meaning the critic wished to examine.[57] The conflict became even more alarming, he thought, when the interpretation of Nature was the question at issue. The natural scientist always ran the risk of opposition from the Church, and when one asked why this should be, the only answer that could be made, Draper felt, was that

some fifteen hundred years ago, there was a Roman general who seized imperial power from his competitors, and whose political necessities were such that he had to inaugurate this untoward course. Because he did it, therefore we must do it![58]

The consequence was that Western Europe labored under the dead weight of vast ecclesiastical establishments. Their influences ramified through all the ranks of society. The Byzantine emperors and the Roman pontiffs had made the Church the determined antagonist of science, a role which enforced its authority and which it was now powerless to abandon. In those countries of Europe where the Church was still dominant, it was inevitable, Draper believed, that "every onward step that science makes implies a conflict."[59] Europe's sorrow, however, was America's opportunity. Free from the dead weight of the Church and with institutions which facilitate rather than resist free thought, the United States ought, said Draper, to stand forth as the defender of freedom.[60]

Draper therefore concluded his analysis of American policy with a chapter on "The Natural Course of National Development," in which he argued that the tendency toward the consolidation of national power following the Civil War was really not the contradiction of the democratic process but its fulfillment. Since all history is moving toward the supremacy of the intellect, one can discover the meaning of history only in those cultures where intellectual development is allowed to proceed without the hindrance of material interests or intrenched institutions.[61] Such conditions exist only in America, which must become in consequence the future battleground of ideas. When the conflict of ideas is permitted to work itself out freely, there emerges a unanimity of opinion, which is well illustrated by the tendency of scientific opinion to achieve the status of law. And what is true of ideas, Draper thought,

[57] *Ibid.*, p. 205. [58] *Ibid.*, pp. 234–35. [59] *Ibid.*, pp. 235–36.
[60] *Ibid.*, p. 213. [61] *Ibid.*, p. 297.

is equally true of social institutions. The creation of national unity and consolidated government was indeed the achievement of Northern arms in the Civil War, but this in turn had been made possible by the dominance of an idea, "that there shall exist on this continent one Republic, great and indivisible,"[62] and by the persistence of a sense of national dedication and purpose, "the sentiment of a manifest destiny to imperial greatness [which] gives to every one a determinate direction and an energetic life."[63] It was clear to Draper that American unity of ideals and uniformity of political institutions alike were the fruit of the American democratic way of life.

Thus the United States, in Draper's opinion, was the nation best suited to resolve the conflict between science and religion because her ideals and institutions both permitted and exemplified the benefits of freedom. Yet Draper was struck by the analogy of the American government and the Roman ecclesiastical system—so much so that he ended his discussion of American civil policy by pointing to the lessons that America could learn from Rome. In the contrast between the two, the Roman and the American systems, Draper could see embodied in institutions the essential conflict between religion and science. Religion, he thought, as represented by the Roman Church was exclusive and partisan, for it sought privileges for a special class in a limited territory affiliated with a particular organization, whereas the government of the United States was national in its loyalties, continental in its extent, and representative of all classes of men. Moreover, the Roman system rested on the supernatural, which, according to Draper, was "in its very nature delusive and unsatisfactory," whereas American republicanism rested on reason, which was enduring.[64] Nevertheless, the Roman Church illustrated in miniature what lines of development the American state might anticipate in the future.

In the history of this wonderful power, that for a thousand years maintained its sway, the American, I repeat, may find abundant instruction. . . . He may see how, in its limited sphere, it depended on the same principles on which he is depending. It signified nothing to the Church that her greatest dignitaries had come from the lowest social ranks. Mental capacity was what she sought; she appropriated it wherever she could find it. Considering the intrinsic weakness of the intellectual basis on which she rested, considering how incompatible it was with increasing enlightenment, our admiration may be worthily excited by the wondrous duration of her power. In that we may perceive auspices of the most favorable kind for ourselves, who likewise are making everything depend on the organization of intellect . . .[65]

[62] *Thoughts on the Future Civil Policy of America*, p. 297.
[63] *Ibid.*, p. 312.
[64] *Ibid.*, p. 317.   [65] *Ibid.*, p. 316.

It was Draper's hope that American power, resting as it did upon science and democracy, would achieve for the modern world the degree of unity and organization which the Church of Rome had effected for the Middle Ages. In the growth of nationalism in the United States he looked forward to the resolution of the antagonism between science and religion.

To illustrate these principles from the recent history of the United States, Draper wrote his most ambitious work, the three-volume *History of the American Civil War*, published between 1867 and 1870. Draper believed that the Civil War had resulted from sectional antagonisms which were themselves caused by natural differences, and that similar antagonisms would appear elsewhere in the United States when sectional interests developed. To recognize that geographic areas and human types produced corresponding political problems, he said, was to realize that only the highest statesmanship, founded on the principle of justice, would preserve the republic.[66]

In his analysis of the lessons of the Civil War, Draper reasserted his governing assumption, that man and history are controlled by natural law, but he argued that this basic truth of science was in no way antagonistic to religion. Individual men and their social groups, it seemed to him, reflected clearly the operation of natural forces, so that a study of men or their communities would reveal the whole course of history. So also the events of history were under the control of natural law rather than individual caprice.

The springs of history are not, as was for a long time imagined, the machinations of statesmen or the ambition of kings. They are to be found in the silent influences of Nature. The philosopher will often detect the true causes of great political and social convulsions, of sectional hatreds and national attachments, in the shining of the sun and in the falling of rains.[67]

Such natural forces, he felt, had been too often overlooked, and he proposed in his history of the Civil War to give them proper attention. A knowledge of the natural conditions of history would help to reinforce the truths of religion because in the light of adequate knowledge men would be inclined to take a more charitable view of the actions of their fellows.

Estimating rightly these things, we are led to entertain more philosophical, more enlarged, more enlightened, and, in truth, more benevolent views of each other's proceedings.[68]

Thus the recognition of the control of natural law would help to reconcile

---

[66] John William Draper, *History of the American Civil War* (New York, 1867–70), I, 29–30.
[67] *Ibid.*, I, 37–38.
[68] *Ibid.*, I, 37.

estrangements which result from a misunderstanding of the proper limits of human freedom.

The greatest lesson to be learned from the War, accordingly, was not so much the inviolability of natural law as man's power through the use of reason to control nature and exert his freedom. Draper refused to accept the assumption that the conflict had been irrepressible, for he believed that with increasing knowledge of its physical causes the sources of sectional antagonism might come within the reach of human control. He turned again to the analogy of intellectual conflicts within the domain of science, where he found that every day was bringing greater unanimity of opinion and a nearer approach to truth.

Then must we submit ourselves unresistingly to the tyranny of Nature [he asked], and accept things as they come with stoical indifference, or Mohammedan resignation? Shall we give up this Union because we see that it is threatened in all directions with dangers? Has not science taught us that we may deliver ourselves from such evils, and increase at once our happiness and power by a right interpretation of Nature—by availing ourselves of the unvarying operation of those laws which we can not directly resist? Opposing conditions we may reconcile; conflicts that are irrepressible we can manage; disasters we may avert, or even turn into blessings.[69]

It was clear to Draper that there was nothing in the creed of the positive scientist to deny human freedom or to assert the fatalistic supremacy of natural law over human destiny.

The conflict of religion and science and the prospect of its resolution was illustrated further, Draper thought, by another problem associated with the Civil War and its aftermath. This was the problem of social conflict resulting from the presence in a community of peoples with different physical constitutions and different cultures. Just as the differences of physical geography produced the conflict of sections, so also the differences of human anthropology produced the conflict of diverse peoples. This was not a new problem nor one peculiar to the United States, Draper pointed out. It strengthened the analogy between the position of the United States in the contemporary world and that of the Church of Rome in the Middle Ages, he thought, to discover that Rome had twice faced the same problem and twice solved it. The Roman Republic, faced with the problem of assimilating her conquests, had solved it by imperialism; the Roman Church, faced with the problem of organizing the fragments of the Roman Empire, had solved it by ecclesiasticism.

[69] *History of the American Civil War*, I, 31.

Although neither of these solutions would now suffice to meet the problem of diverse peoples in America, a third solution in accord with American principles was gradually emerging: the extension of universal education and with it the "organization of the intelligence of the nation" for the guidance of public affairs. In schemes for competitive examination he thought he could see prospects for the reforms of the civil service, which would check the evils of the spoils system and make talent and experience available for the benefit of the republic.[70] And it would be necessary further, Draper thought, judging from the experience of Europe, to nationalize the telegraph and the railroad, in order that the systems for the transmission of intelligence should not fall into private hands.[71] Thus the means now available to the American people for solving the problem of racial diversity as of geographical difference were means which science had provided. This fact made it more clearly apparent to Draper that no solution devised in a "prescientific" age was applicable to the current problem as it existed in America. Tyranny would follow an attempt to impose either of the Roman solutions, imperialism or ecclesiasticism. Indeed, the essential conflict between science and religion, Draper was now coming to see, was the conflict between a set of social instituitions which had now long outlived their usefulness and a system of social organization implicit in the methods and findings of science.

Draper therefore identified the victory of the North in the Civil War with the cause of science. Science had organized the resources of the North for victory; science had provided the network of railroads by means of which the Northern armies had conducted their operations on two fronts. So it seemed an inescapable conclusion that the political consequences of the war were themselves illustrations of fundamental scientific propositions. For one thing, the triumph of nationality over the principle of states rights, although perhaps a contradiction of the Constitution as it was originally understood, was consistent with the tendency of scientific knowledge toward unity and uniformity.[72] The Northern victory, moreover, was a triumph for the notion of progress. This was a conception, he believed, as characteristically American as reverence for the past was characteristically Roman. Like science itself, "the American forgets the past, is dissatisfied with the present, and lives for the future."[73] The outcome of the Civil War could be expected, he thought, to put an end to the conflict between science and religion because it had demonstrated at such a cost in blood and tears the validity of central scientific assump-

[70] *Ibid.*, III, 665–66.   [71] *Ibid.*, III, 672.
[72] *Ibid.*, III, 673.   [73] *Ibid.*, III, 675.

tions. Draper concluded, somewhat overoptimistically, that even the South would come in time to acknowledge the divine judgment in the Northern victory, seeing the accomplishment of emancipation and the establishment of nationality "not as the victory of the North, but as the fiat of God."[74]

After the Vatican Council of 1870 announced the doctrine of papal infallibility, Draper in his last work turned his attention directly to the question of the conflict of science and religion and undertook to put it in its proper historical setting. In the ensuing book, published in 1873 under the title, *History of the Conflict Between Religion and Science*, he examines six historic conflicts, among them the conflict respecting the nature of the soul, the conflict respecting the nature of the world, and the controversy respecting the government of the universe; and he concludes with an analysis of the relation of science and of Christianity to modern civilization and a statement of the nature of the current crisis between them.

Draper now regarded the relationship between science and religion primarily as a contest between two forms of power: science, he thought, represented the forces of progress, intelligence, and freedom; religion, especially Roman Catholicism, those of retrogression, bigotry, and slavery. He believed that Western society faced a crisis in which "the intellectual basis of faith has been undermined by the spirit of the age."[75] From the presuppositions of the Roman Catholics, at least, he was certain that the conflict was an irreconcilable one: "Roman Christianity and Science are recognized by their respective adherents as being absolutely incompatible: they cannot exist together; one must yield to the other; mankind must make its choice—it cannot have both."[76] But although Draper did not believe that any reconciliation was possible for the Roman Catholic, he thought there might be one for the Protestant, who, through the doctrine of private interpretation of the Scriptures, could restore the friendship between science and religion which "misunderstandings have alienated."

Science and religion were fundamentally in conflict, he believed, because religion maintained its power through the rigid institutional structure of the Church, claiming for it a divine sanction, whereas science sought to destroy the Church's pretension to power by demonstrating its human origins. Draper anticipated the later social Darwinists by emphasizing the fact of social change. He contrasted faith and science in terms of their teachings about the develop-

---

[74] *History of the American Civil War*, III, 676.

[75] John William Draper, *History of the Conflict Between Religion and Science* (New York, 1873), p. 274.

[76] *Ibid.*, p. 303.

ment of society. Religion, he wrote, is "in its nature unchangeable, stationary," whereas science is "in its nature progressive."[77] In the resulting conflict science is allied with the "expansive force of the human intellect" while religion represents the "compression arising from traditionary faith." This explained, it seemed to him, why in history the Church had everywhere opposed free scientific inquiry. It also explained why the Church now opposed progress. For its part in the Holy Inquisition, Draper arraigned the Church as an institution which used the civil power to retard progress, and asserted that science, on the other hand, "has never sought to ally herself to civil power."[78]

It was Draper's contention that the Church depended upon its power as an institution to maintain its dogma, which, if left unsupported by artificial means, would crumble naturally from the undermining of science. Hence the conflict between science and religion was the opposition of reason and faith: whereas Roman Catholicism claimed the supremacy of faith, science asserted the supremacy of reason. Since he felt that no compromise was possible between such antagonistic claims, he concluded that "faith must render an account of herself to reason." Because he had found the claims of faith associated throughout history with fiction and fraud and organized impostures and delusions, he could not admit the validity of arguments in their favor.[79] He contended, moreover, that the Roman Church had repudiated its own position by appealing to reason to support its claims while denouncing reason as a possible judge in its dispute with science.

Draper, for his part, repudiated the papal claim to infallibility because he did not see how it could be applied to matters of faith and morals and withheld in questions of science. This ambiguous position had resulted, he thought, in the antagonism between science and religion, which threatened to overwhelm Western society.

An impassable and hourly-widening gulf [Draper wrote] intervenes between Catholicism and the spirit of the age. Catholicism insists that blind faith is superior to reason; that mysteries are of more importance than facts. She claims to be the sole interpreter of Nature and revelation, the supreme arbiter of knowledge; she summarily rejects all modern criticism of the Scriptures, and orders the Bible to be accepted in accordance with the views of the theologians of Trent; she openly avows her hatred of free institutions and constitutional systems, and declares that those are in damnable error who regard the reconciliation of the pope with modern civilization as ether possible or desirable.[80]

77 *Ibid.*, p. x.
78 *Ibid.*, p. xiii.
79 *Ibid.*, p. 306.
80 *Ibid.*, p. 302.

Draper saw little hope out of this impasse short of the destruction of ecclesiastical power and religious pretension—no hope at all on the basis of Roman Catholic dogma and very little hope even from the standpoint of the Protestant reliance upon the right of private judgment. But science, he believed, would stand firm amid the ruins of churches and creeds. He explained that science was even then calling into the conflict new rivals to Christianity. He observed the impact upon Western society of distant and different religious systems— "the Mohammedan, the Buddhist, the Brahman"—and he predicted that Christianity would suffer the fate of Roman paganism, while science alone would surmount the religious crisis because science "has given us grander views of the universe, more awful views of God."[81] Thus the pretensions of the Roman Catholic Church had done untold disservice, he felt, to the cause of religion and had retarded the possible reconciliation of science and religion. The triumph of American nationality had provided fertile soil for the development of a religion of science, but by the early 1870's it looked to Draper as if this could be accomplished only by the destruction of Roman Catholic power.

[81] *History of the Conflict Between Religion and Science*, p. xiii.

3

Social Darwinism
Andrew Dickson White and John Fiske

ANDREW D. WHITE's *History of the Warfare of Science with Theology in Christendom*, the outcome of two decades of lecturing and writing on the problem of the relationship of science and religion, was published in 1896. White had first entered the lists with an address at Cooper Union in New York entitled "The Battle-Fields of Science." There he had maintained the thesis that free scientific enquiry always operated to the benefit of both religion and science, while religious interference uniformly worked to their injury.[1] In 1877 this address was expanded and published in a booklet entitled *The Warfare of Science*. White next turned to the project of writing a series of articles on the same theme for *Popular Science Monthly*. In the preparation of material for these articles, he enlisted the services of George Lincoln Burr, formerly his student at Cornell and later his colleague. These articles, revised and expanded, became the two-volume *History*. The success of the work was instantaneous. It captured the anticlerical sentiment of the *fin de siècle* 'nineties, and provided for a generation the platform for the nineteenth-century crusade against Roman Catholicism, Protestant fundamentalism, and ecclesiasticism generally.[2]

White's analysis of the relationship between science and religion came at the end of the generation that Draper began. His book continues the attack upon the same enemy, entrenched ecclesiasticism, but it fails to maintain the fundamental antagonisms of Draper's work. Yet it shows clearly the extent to which the evolutionary concept had found its way, from Spencer through John Fiske, into the American mind. A comparison of the two works leaves the impression that White makes a less convincing case for science than Draper had a quarter-century before. The differences between White's *Warfare* and Draper's *Conflict* weaken rather than strengthen the position of the critic of religion. These differences may be reduced to three propositions which temper

---

[1] *A History of the Warfare of Science with Theology in Christendom*, I, viii.

[2] Bainton, *George Lincoln Burr*, p. 49. In the spring of 1910 Burr, as librarian of the President White Library, reported to White that the receipts were already over $7,000. In 1924 the book still brought in $402 (*ibid.*, p. 52).

and modify the impact of science and religion which Draper had affirmed in unequivocal terms.

In the first place, White sees the conflict much more completely in its historic context than had Draper. The conflict between science and religion is a conflict between the modern world and the medieval world. "More and more," he wrote, "I saw that it was the conflict between two epochs in human thought—the theological and the scientific."[3] The mission of science in the modern world was to disprove the dogma of the Middle Ages. White maintained that medieval attitudes and ideas continued to exist, to the detriment and embarassment of modern thought, and he stated that his purpose was to let "the light of historical truth into that decaying mass of outworn thought which attaches the modern world to medieval conceptions of Christianity . . ."[4] The formulation in historic terms of the conflict between religion and science led White throughout his book to make an age rather than an institution the object of his attack. The pattern of medieval society shows the depths to which a civilization, unmindful of the insights and methods of science, can fall. But the temptation to give a historical locus to the enemies of scientific advance marks a retreat from the more uncompromising position of Draper.

If the Middle Ages was the peculiar target of modern science, it followed that religion was to be condemned only to the extent that it exhibited qualities peculiarly medieval. This meant that the conflict with science did not involve religion generally, but only medieval religion. This was the second significant point of difference between White's position and Draper's.

. . . I admired Draper's treatment of the questions involved [White wrote], [but] his point of view and mode of looking at history were different from mine.

He regarded the struggle as one between Science and Religion. I believed then, and am convinced now, that it was a struggle between Science and Dogmatic Theology.[5]

In making the distinction between "dogmatic theology," which was central to the medieval system, and "religion pure and undefiled," which was not antagonistic to science, White was not interested primarily in the emancipation of religion. For twenty years he had been fighting sectarian control at Cornell, and in his attempts to associate the sciences, the humanities, and religion he had been forced to answer charges of infidelity leveled against his administration. His major interest, as Draper's, was the liberation of science,

---

[3] White, *op. cit.*, I, ix.
[4] *Ibid.*, I, v–vi.   [5] *Ibid.*, I, ix.

but this he thought possible without the complete destruction of religion. Only dogma, unreason, and outworn thought need be liquidated in the process.

The warfare between science and theology which White described developed through three stages. In the first stage, a new scientific discovery was attacked in the name of the Scriptures. This battle lost, theology retired to the inner defenses of dogma. But under the attack of science, even the bulwarks of dogma must crumble, until, in the third stage, theology is forced to compromise as a prelude to capitulation. But the defeat of theology is held to liberate religion as well as science:

. . . modern science, in substituting a new heaven and a new earth for the old—the reign of law for the reign of caprice, and the idea of evolution for that of creation—has added and is steadily adding a new revelation divinely inspired.[6]

The revelation of science strengthened rather than weakened religion. Freed from its incubus of unreasoning dogma and its subservience to "Biblical texts and ancient modes of thought," it could march hand in hand with science toward a future of service if not of faith. Such a religion White would define in terms of "the recognition of 'a Power in the universe, not ourselves, which makes for righteousness,' and in the love of God and of our neighbor . . ."[7] In this respect, also, White withdrew from the more positive position of Draper.

A third point of difference between White's analysis and that of Draper was his emphasis upon the place of evolution in mitigating the conflict and in determining its eventual outcome. The passage from the medieval to the modern epoch had been accomplished within the pattern of the evolutionary hypothesis. White noted among his many applications of the doctrine of evolution to history the shift of control in education in both Europe and America from the clergy to the laity. This proved, he thought, "the continuance of that evolution which I have endeavored to describe in this series of monographs—an evolution, indeed, in which the warfare of Theology against Science has been one of the most active and powerful agents."[8] Thus the conflict between science and dogmatic theology was itself an instrument of progress. The ultimate meaning and significance, however, of the doctrine of evolution was that it provided a basis for the eventual reconciliation of science and religion, for both were subject to the inexorable operation of its laws. Religious literature and doctrine could be acknowledged as true in the sense that they were documents "of the evolving heart, mind, and soul of man."[9] To mitigate the

6 Ibid., I, 23–24.   7 Ibid., I, xii.   8 Ibid., I, xi–xii.   9 Ibid., I, 23.

conflict it was necessary to recognize that science and theology apply to different data, but that these data are amenable in being responsible to the same laws. There are two evolutions, White maintained, one of the natural universe, the other of a "sacred creation-legend."

The warfare of science with theology was one which, from White's point of view, had been largely won with the evolution from medieval to modern times. On what terms, then, might science and religion be expected to exist without conflict in the modern world? White was not only convinced that the reconciliation was possible, but he thought it could be achieved soon. He asserted, to begin with, that scientific doctrine and its formulation were divinely inspired—a new revelation to be substituted for the creation story of the Bible. From this point of view the discoveries of science were thought to sustain rather than to undermine man's faith in a divinely established order. It was clear that he left no room for a distinction between the acquisition of knowledge and the apprehension of values.

Again, White proposed that the reconciliation should be achieved through the renunciation by the clergy of questions of faith and doctrine for programs of social service.

My belief is that in the field left to them—their proper field—the clergy will more and more, as they cease to struggle against scientific methods and conclusions, do work even nobler and more beautiful than anything they have heretofore done.[10]

This view, which was commonly held during the first three decades of the twentieth century, helped to emasculate the social gospel movement of much of its intellectual force.

In the third place, White agreed with the social Darwinists of his generation in looking to the doctrine of evolution for an answer to all questions. Evolution was the master key of the universe which would unlock truths so universal that they would dissolve all elements of controversy between science and religion. It should have been apparent that if religion itself is subject to the determinisms of Nature, it necessarily and inevitably loses its power to work transformations for righteousness in men's lives. The accommodation of religion to the patterns of the contingent world obscured the elements of absolutism in every genuinely religious insight by virtue of which it undertakes to make the force of its idealism felt in the world.

And finally, White based his optimism upon the security of middle-class privileges, which, more than all else, distinguished the modern world from

[10] White, *op. cit.*, I, xii.

the Middle Ages. One of the principal foundations, he thought, for the stability and progress of the modern world was the system of free business enterprise. Until the relaxation of the medieval strictures upon usury, a free economy could not become established. In the release of economic individualism, his argument ran, two forces were necessary—science, which repudiated the method of the scholastic defenders of ecclesiastical privilege, and the Protestant revolution, which challenged the authority of the Church itself. For centuries the opposition of the Church to productive investment had sharpened the conflict between religion and science, but with this battle won the way was open for a reconciliation.[11] But the repudiation of medieval economic control went further than the defense of accepting interest, for White failed to appreciate the ideal which inspired the medieval welfare economy. He saw that the evolution of modern society had accomplished the substitution of modern poor relief—"the idea that men are to be helped to help themselves"—for medieval charity—"indiscriminate giving." His inability to recognize the primacy of Christian love, wherever it is found, vitiates his reconciliation of science with a "religion" which rests neither on doctrine nor on charity. White's judgment upon the contribution of science to the Christian life, that "scientific modes of thought in social science have given a new and nobler fruitage to the whole growth of Christian benevolence,"[12] documents rather the religious insensitivity of America in the 1890's than the insight of the apologist of science.

For the last quarter of the nineteenth century no man did more to popularize the doctrine of evolution and to bring it into harmony with current religious ideas than John Fiske, sometime Harvard professor, platform lecturer, social philosopher, and historian. Fiske was the first American to attempt a systematic elucidation of Herbert Spencer's *Synthetic Philosophy*, and from the publication of his two-volume *Outlines of Cosmic Philosophy* in 1874 until the appearance in 1899 and 1900 of his divinity school lectures at Cambridge, under the titles of *The Idea of God as Affected by Modern Knowledge*, *The Idea of Immortality*, and *Through Nature to God*, he remained the foremost apostle of Darwinism in America.

The whole temper and spirit of Fiske's attack upon the problem of the relationship of science and religion differed markedly from that of Draper and White. The genial and kindly Fiske showed nothing of the acerbity which had marked Draper's *Conflict* and White's *Warfare* with iconoclasm.

[11] *Ibid.*, II, 264–76.   [12] *Ibid.*, II, 287.

Instead of calling for the destruction of ecclesiasticism and dogma by the weapons of scientific inquiry, Fiske tried to show not only that the antagonists could be reconciled, but that there was not even an issue to divide them, much less to bring them to battle. For although his main interest was to acquaint the Americans of his generation with the leading features of the Darwinian hypothesis, he showed no desire to weaken the claims of religion or to supplant its doctrines. On the contrary, his discussions of the relationship between science and religion are informed by a desire to strengthen and rehabilitate the claims of contemporary Christianity. His religious writing is, therefore, illuminated throughout by a substratum of fundamental Christian assumptions which give plausibility to the social Darwinism which forms its context. But the Christian doctrine in his writing is not sufficiently emphatic to save it from submergence in the nature philosophy which everywhere rationalized the social anarchism of late nineteenth-century society. All that remains, after Fiske has surrendered to the ideas of immanent deity and uniform nature, is the hope with which he began: that the hostility between science and religion may cease and that thinking it away will really accomplish its dissipation.[13]

The conflict between science and religion is a fanciful one, and it will disappear when men recognize that the essential conflict is one which does not really involve religion as a contestant at all. Why, then, has any appearance of hostility in fact emerged? Fiske offers three explanations. For one thing, Western theology is so completely dominated by the Augustinian conception of God that theists and atheists alike assume it, and it lies at the basis of the orthodoxy of the one and of the iconoclasm of the other, even though they would quickly repudiate it as an explicit dogma. This doctrine is

the idea of a Being actuated by human passions and purposes, localizable in space and utterly remote from that inert machine, the universe in which we live, and upon which He acts intermittently through the suspension of what are called natural laws.

The fact that this conception of deity is so widely held is responsible, Fiske believed, for "that complicated misunderstanding which, by a lamentable confusion of thought, is commonly called 'the conflict between religion and science.' "[14]

From this idea of God it followed as a consequence that the realms of

[13] John Fiske, *Outlines of Cosmic Philosophy, Based on the Doctrine of Evolution, with Criticisms on the Positive Philosophy*, I, xii.

[14] John Fiske, *The Idea of God as Affected by Modern Knowledge*, pp. 95–96.

natural law and of divine action were necessarily disassociated, so that an explanation of the regular and recurring phenomena of the one had no place amid the capricious and heterogeneous phenomena of the other. "This antithesis," Fiske wrote, "has forever haunted the minds of men imbued with the lower or Augustinian theism," and has tended further to arouse the hostility toward each other of theologians and men of science.[15]

A third explanation was the tendency among persons whose moral life is organized around old familiar theories to oppose new ideas for fear that their acceptance would "in some way lower men's standard of life, and make them less careful of their spiritual welfare." Fiske could recognize the honesty of such an argument, since, unlike a misunderstanding of the issues or a determination to maintain a privileged position, it opposed scientific conclusions "on religious grounds, and not simply from mental dulness or rigidity." To the extent, then, that resistance to scientific innovation was prompted by religious feeling it might be said that a conflict between science and religion actually existed.[16] But in no case was the conflict necessary or inevitable, and one might rely with confidence upon the sweet light of reason to dissolve it.

It was as a rational hypothesis of universal applicability, then, that Fiske related the doctrine of evolution to the conflict between science and religion. In this respect its function was identical with that claimed for positivism by Comte: to turn science from the repudiation of religious dogma to the construction of a great synthesis of all scientific knowledge upon which a new theory of religion and of society might ultimately rest.[17] The doctrine of evolution, Fiske believed, was a truth of the widest generalization yet reached by man concerning the concrete universe as a whole. This doctrine he thought equally applicable to the phenomena of science and of religion. Within its embracing arms the interrelationship of all the sciences could be achieved— the realization of Bacon's prophetic dream of an organic philosophy in which all branches of knowledge would have their place as members of the whole. "Such a result," Fiske maintained, "is entitled *par excellence* to the name Cosmic Philosophy."[18]

The universe as comprehended by the general view of cosmism exhibited as its leading characteristics the qualities of unity and of order. The first made the cosmist an uncompromising monotheist. "For what," Fiske asks,

[15] *Ibid.*, p. 107.

[16] John Fiske, "Draper on Science and Religion" (November 1875), in *The Unseen World and Other Essays*, p. 190.

[17] *Outlines of Cosmic Philosophy*, II, 487.

[18] *Ibid.*, I, 276.

"is the philosophic purport of these beautiful and sublime discoveries with which the keen insight and patient diligence of modern students of science are beginning to be rewarded?" The answer is the lesson of the unity of nature, which so intimately relates all the things that we can see and know "that nothing could be left out without reducing the whole marvellous scheme to chaos."[19] And against the claim that the doctrine of evolution substituted, for the divine order, an order of nature, he asserted that the position of the "consistent theist" was "impregnable" in holding that the whole series of natural phenomena connected in terms of the Darwinian hypothesis was rightly "an immediate manifestation of the creative action of God."[20]

In terms of the theory of evolution, then, the final reconciliation between science and religion is essayed by Fiske from two directions. In the first place, evolution is the mechanism which explains alike the development of the truth of science and the teachings of religion. Both conform to the same cosmic process and issue from the same cause. And second, under the harmonizing influence of the evolutionary process, both science and religion work toward the same ends.

The first argument, Fiske believes, effectively refutes the claims of materialism and establishes a scientific foundation for belief in God. "Our common sense argument," he wrote in a late work,

puts the scientific presumption entirely and decisively on the side of religion and against all atheistic and materialistic explanations of the universe. It establishes harmony between our highest knowledge and our highest aspirations by showing that the latter no less than the former are a normal result of the universal cosmic process. It has nothing to fear from the advance of scientific discovery, for as these things come to be better understood, it is going to be realized that the days of the antagonism between Science and Religion must by and by come to an end. That antagonism has been chiefly due to the fact that religious ideas were until lately allied with the doctrine of special creations. They have therefore needed to be remodelled and considered from new points of view. But we have at length reached a stage where it is becoming daily more and more apparent that with the deeper study of Nature the old strife between faith and knowledge is drawing to a close; and disentangled at last from that ancient slough of despond the Human mind will breathe a freer air and enjoy a vastly extended horizon.[21]

The second argument, that science and religion serve the same ends, helps to reconcile the conflicting claims of matter and spirit. Each must be

---

[19] John Fiske, *Through Nature to God*, pp. 23–24.

[20] John Fiske, "Darwinism Verified" (December 1876), in *Darwinism and Other Essays*, pp. 6–7.

[21] *Through Nature to God*, pp. 193–94.

pushed to its inevitable conclusion, and then it will appear that both are united in an "enduring alliance" to do battle for "the same eternal cause—the cause of truth, of goodness, and of beauty; 'the glory of God, and the relief of man's estate.' "[22] Science and religion are thus united by the evolutionary doctrine at both ends of the cosmic process, for they proceed from the same cause and work toward the same result. It remains to show how Fiske uses this doctrine to bring science and religion to terms in dealing with the problems of the nature of God, the meaning of the moral life, and the possibility of knowledge.

Fiske rests much of his argument for the concord of science and religion upon the proposition that both disciplines establish the same deity. Not only does science affirm the existence of God, but also the God of science is really the God which religion, when purged of its mythological encrustations, affirms. Dogmatic theology, unfortunately, has traditionally presented the Deity in personal terms, overtly asserting the infinitude and omnipotence of God, while tacitly belying this acknowledgment "by the implication, which runs through all its reasonings, that God is a person localized in some unknown part of space, and that the universe is a 'datum objective to God' in somewhat the same sense that a steam-engine is an 'objective datum' to the engineer who works it."[23] Hence, the real antagonists in the struggle to free the human mind are not science and religion but cosmism and anthropomorphism. Fiske's task in liberating man's intelligence is thus to "deanthropomorphize" his conception of the Deity and to substitute for it the Power which cosmism "refrains from defining and limiting by metaphysical formulas, thereby acknowledging so far as the exigencies of human speaking and thinking will allow—that it is infinite and absolute."[24] In this way, Fiske believes, the cosmic philosophy will "utterly and for ever" sweep away "the apparent antagonism between Science and Religion, which is the abiding terror of timid or superficial minds . . ."

The conception of God which emerges from this analysis emphasizes the infinity of the Deity and its immanence in the phenomena of the world of nature.

There exists a POWER [Fiske asserts], to which no limit in time or space is conceivable, of which all phenomena, as presented in consciousness, are manifestations, but which we can know only through these manifestations. Here is a formula legitimately obtained by the employment of scientific methods, as the last result

[22] *Outlines of Cosmic Philosophy*, II, 508.
[23] *Ibid.*, II, 425.
[24] *Ibid.*, I, 184.

of a subjective analysis on the one hand, and of an objective analysis on the other hand.[25]

But God, as thus conceived, is no different from the Deity which man's basic religious inclinations support and justify:

. . . this formula, which presents itself as the final outcome of a purely scientific inquiry, expresses also the fundamental truth of Theism,—the truth by which religious feeling is justified. The existence of God—the supreme truth asserted alike by Christianity and by inferior historic religions—is asserted with equal emphasis by that Cosmic Philosophy which seeks its data in science alone.[26]

The God of cosmism, however, is not the Unknowable of Spencer, for it is revealed "in every pulsation of the wondrously rich and beautiful life of the Universe."[27] Indeed, Fiske goes to the extent of claiming for scientific thought that it brings forth an idea of God that is "practically identical with the Athanasian conception of the immanent Deity."

One of the most serious consequences of the anthropomorphic conception of God was, in Fiske's view, the separation of the domain of natural law from the realm of divine action. This would seem to withdraw the world of natural phenomena from the province of divine meaning and thereby establish the presuppositions on the basis of which a conflict between science and religion becomes necessary and inevitable. But to avoid this hiatus in the phenomena of experience it was necessary, he thought, merely to affirm with the cosmist that God was immanent in nature. The cosmist will exclude God from no part of the world; he will acknowledge "no such inherent and incurable viciousness in the constitution of things" as the anthropomorphic hypothesis postulates.[28] Instead, he will endorse the "higher theism" of Clement and Athanasius, adopt the conception of an ever present God, and recognize the fact, now become self-evident, "that the law of gravitation is but an expression of a particular mode of divine action."[29]

Granted that the God of science is truly the God of religion and that the natural world is an expression of the divine purpose, it remains to be shown that the cosmos, so understood, is consistent with the highest moral principles advanced by religion and ethics. Fiske maintained not only that the ethical code deduced from his analysis of the cosmic process was identical with that

[25] *Outlines of Cosmic Philosophy*, II, 415.

[26] *Ibid.*, II, 415.

[27] *Through Nature to God*, p. 150.

[28] *Outlines of Cosmic Philosophy*, II, 429.

[29] *The Idea of God*, pp. 109–10.

of the "highest Christianity,"[30] but also that its sanctions were more powerful and its theoretical basis "incomparably deeper and stronger" than those of the traditional religion.[31] How was this possible? His explanation is in terms of a biological naturalism centering in the doctrine of evolution. According to Fiske, the theory of Darwinism proved that the modifications necessary to ensure the survival of a species were just those which contributed to the ultimate welfare of the species. Ultimate welfare was in fact the determining element in the selection of those modifications which would enable the species to survive.[32] Applied to human morals, this doctrine affirmed a hierarchy of moral claims beginning with the ultimate salvation of mankind and ending with the individual's adjustment to the requirements of nature. In effecting this cosmic design, man is obliged to obey a religious instinct which has its source in the rectitude and happiness of the community and its end in the conformity of man to the mechanisms and demands of the natural world.[33] In this analysis Fiske emphasizes man's responsiveness to a cosmic purpose rather than his subservience to individual biologic needs. The *Cosmic Philosophy* is primarily a philosophy of the macrocosm, not the microcosm. It is integrative rather than analytical, for it initiates the stream of causation in the universal organism—which is God—rather than in the isolated phenomenon of nature. Man's moral life, therefore, takes on meaning because it is an expression of cosmic purpose.

If science and religion can be reconciled at the different levels of God and of the moral life, so also can a reconciliation be accomplished in the area of human knowledge. Indeed, much of the conflict has arisen, he believes, from an inadequate recognition of the fact that science and religion perform different functions in the search for truth, functions which, if properly conceived, involve no conflict whatever. "The business of science," he maintained repeatedly, "is simply to ascertain in what manner phenomena co-exist with each other or follow each other . . ."[34] If there appears to be a conflict, it arises from a failure to recognize that the advance guard of scientific knowledge is always involved in a struggle to maintain itself against the cruder science of yesterday. Sometimes, indeed, religious orthodoxy becomes associated with the repudiated hypotheses of science, such as the doctrine of special creation.

[30] *Outlines of Cosmic Philosophy*, II, 506.

[31] *Ibid.*, II, 468.

[32] John Fiske, "Evolution and the Present Age," in *Essays Historical and Literary* (New York, 1902), II, 284.

[33] *Outlines of Cosmic Philosophy*, II, 502.

[34] "Darwinism Verified," in *Darwinism and Other Essays*, p. 7; *The Idea of God*, pp. 101–2.

In such an event the response of science and religion alike should not be a declaration of war but rather a common dedication to the task of purging commonly held religious conceptions of their vestiges of mythology.[35]

Having restricted their respective fields of operation, science and religion can strengthen and perpetuate their alliance by embracing the insights of the evolutionist. The extension of the methods of science to wider areas will help to dispel the errors of fact which are, in part, the basis of the hostility between science and religion.[36] Moreover, the methods of science emphasize the tentativity of all knowledge, holding that all opinions are held subject to continual revision, whereas the essential articles of faith make their claims absolutely. Thus the realms of knowledge and of dogma are further differentiated, leaving religion in sole possession of all propositions which claim more than a merely relative truth. Fiske raises this observation to the level of "an all-important theorem in which science and religion are reconciled," which issues not in atheism or positivism, but in a theism which is "higher and purer, because relatively truer," than the traditional anthropomorphism of the theologians.[37] But that the transition from anthropomorphism to cosmism would necessarily be a slow one Fiske knew. Meanwhile, it was incumbent upon the scientist to look with tolerance upon the views of traditional religion, even though the scrutiny of analytical science might reveal errors and inconsistencies as yet unexpunged from the body of theological dogma. The best way for the scientist to purify theology, it seemed to him, was to press forward his inquiries into the world of nature which at every step affirmed more emphatically the immanence of God.[38] The evolutionist had nothing to fear from the reluctance of the religious mind to surrender its traditional dogma, however slow and painful the process might appear. Moreover, Fiske recognized the virtue of faith as an integrating ideal around which the human personality must organize its life. He believed that "even an unscientific faith [was] infinitely better than an aimless scepticism," and consequently urged the cosmist to refrain from the violent criticism which might result in the destruction of standards.

Fiske's most significant contribution to the history of the relationship of science and religion, however, is not to be found in his application of the doctrine of evolution to the problems of God, of morals, and of knowledge.

---

[35] "Draper on Science and Religion," in *The Unseen World and Other Essays*, p. 191.

[36] *Outlines of Cosmic Philosophy*, II, 499–500.

[37] *Ibid.*, II, pp. 411–12; "Draper on Science and Religion," in *The Unseen World and Other Essays*, p. 192.

[38] *Through Nature to God*, p. xii.

His importance lies in the fact that he could not obscure his sensitivity to essential Christian insights within the structure of social Darwinism which he erected for his philosophic system. Over and over again, Fiske leaves the deterministic presuppositions of nineteenth-century science to place emphasis with unfailing accuracy upon Christian fundamentals. Although he endorses the idea of progress as "on the whole the most constant and prominent feature of the history of a considerable and important portion of mankind,"[39] he makes it clear that the fundamental characteristic of social progress is its moral character and that progress is to be measured by the substitution of sympathy for selfishness.[40] He praises the extension of Roman rule over the Mediterranean, but he states that its consequence was the growth of peace and human equality, culminating in the genesis of Christianity.[41] And he asserts that so far as religious sentiment is concerned, the real struggle is not with science, but "with the selfish propensities whose tendency is to make men lead the lives of brutes."[42] He fully and explicitly embraces the Christian ideal, although he sees the hiatus between Christian possibilities and Christian pretensions, and he rightly strikes at the presumption of Christian theologians in claiming perfect knowledge or complete truth. The theologian, as much as the scientist, obscured the search for truth by asserting his dogmas with an absolutism and finality inconsistent with the state of imperfection in which man finds himself in nature and history.[43] Fiske was aware of man's pretensions, and he called on scientist and theologian alike to work humbly to purge their truths of elements of error. And finally, he touched Christian metaphysics at a vital point. He insisted upon the urgency of maintaining the distinction between ideas and the external facts which they undertake to interpret. He knew that external nature was a fact and that successful living was largely dependent upon the adequacy of adjustment to it.[44] He did not associate the dualism implicit in this position with the distinction between God and the world, or between God and man, probably because he was more particularly concerned with attacking the mechanistic theology which separated God from the universe as the mechanic from the machine. But in a period characterized by the tendency of the current idealism to make nature a product of mind and of the popular materialism to make mind a function of

[39] *Outlines of Cosmic Philosophy*, II, 192.
[40] *Ibid.*, II, 201.
[41] *Ibid.*, II, 206.
[42] "Draper on Science and Religion," in *The Unseen World and Other Essays*, p. 192.
[43] *Outlines of Cosmic Philosophy*, II, 502–3.
[44] *Through Nature to God*, p. 185.

nature, it is worth noting that Fiske preserved an area of independence and freedom for man by disassociating him from the phenomena of nature with which he had to deal.

But with all his awareness of such Christian presuppositions as the primacy of love and the objectivity of the created world, Fiske nevertheless retains an unresolved residue of Nature philosophy, which tends to rob man of his freedom and truth of its validity. For one thing, he does not adequately separate man from the vitalities of nature, with the result that he frequently explains morality as a simple accommodation to Nature. Thus, "that is right which tends to enhance the fulness of life, and that is wrong which tends to detract from fulness of life," with the result that the distinction between right and wrong becomes rooted in the cosmic process rather than in the realm of man's freedom.[45] This doctrine reaches frightening proportions when Fiske robs the moral act in its historic inception of every vestige of self-consciousness. Primitive men, he asserts, first began to shape their conduct with reference to a standard outside of self without "any realizing sense of what they were doing," for the results of evolution steal upon the world noiselessly and unobserved.

The moral law grew up in the world not because anybody asked for it, but because it was needed for the world's work. If it is not a product of the cosmic process, it would be hard to find anything that could be so called.[46]

It is obvious that such a view of morality is meaningless from the Christian standpoint, according to which man achieves morality through a free and knowing response to an act of grace.

Again, Fiske sometimes obscures his theory of moral progress with the view that progress is the development of structure rather than the growth of unselfishness. Here he falls victim to the attempt of the anthropologist to explain the growth of civilization in terms of primitive forms and institutions.[47] But more serious is his distinction between science and religion as realms of the known and of the unknown, instead of the more fruitful distinction, to which he alludes, as the areas of the relative and of the absolute. He claims that the object of worship has from the beginning been "the mys-

[45] John Fiske, "Evolution and Religion" (November 1882), in *Excursions of an Evolutionist* (Boston, 1883), p. 304.

[46] *Through Nature to God*, p. 108.

[47] *Outlines of Cosmic Philosophy*, II, 195. Fiske quotes with approval: "In the science of history, therefore, old 'means not old in chronology, but in structure: that is most archaic which lies nearest to the beginning of human progress considered as a development, and that is most modern which is farthest removed from that beginning'" (M'Lennan, *Primitive Marriage*, p. 9).

terious aspect of things," into which the progress of science has been continually pressing, converting the unknown into the known. But since the advance of knowledge does not diminish the unknown but rather extends it, the place of religion he thinks is secure.[48] The worship of the mysterious in experience quickly transforms a religion of faith into a sentimental mysticism without a body of positive belief. In the attempt to remedy this loss, he took the next logical step and converted the worship of mystery into the worship of mere force or power. The "ultimate mystery" becomes an "omnipresent Energy," before which men of science, now in the presence of the "mystery of mysteries," must reverently pause.

Here religon must ever hold sway, reminding us that from birth until death we are dependent on a Power to whose eternal decrees we must resign ourslves, and upon whose constancy we may implicitly rely.[49]

It would be difficult to find a clearer illustration of the easy transition from science to mystery to power to surrender. If the reconciliation between science and religion is to be made according to this progression, the concept of human freedom quickly loses all significance and the inquiry into the tension of mystery and meaning degenerates into a defense of the established order. Thus in the last of his treatises on the religion of nature Fiske reaches the conclusion that the sorrow, pain, and evil of the world are firmly grounded in the very structure of the cosmos.

In a happy world there must be sorrow and pain, and in a moral world the knowledge of evil is indispensable. The stern necessity for this has been proved to inhere in the innermost constitution of the human soul. It is part and parcel of the universe.[50]

But this was the very crux of the problem of the relationship between science and religion. The central fact for which an adequate religion seeks an explanation is the tragedy of evil. The only solution within the competence of the cosmic philosophy was to fall back into the inevitabilities of nature, which, of course, was no solution at all.

[48] *Outlines of Cosmic Philosophy*, II, 420–21.
[49] *Ibid.*, II, 422.
[50] *Through Nature to God*, p. 37.

4

The Rediscovery of Human Personality
William James

AT THE TURN of the century, the reaction against the easy accommodation of religious phenomena to the processes of natural science had begun in America. It was most clearly voiced by William James, whose scientific training under Agassiz at Harvard and later medical studies combined with work in philosophy in Germany to give him an unrivaled insight into the relationship of science and religion. The position which James took in *The Principles of Psychology*, published in 1890, that religious experience attested the reality of an unseen world beyond the competence of the methods of investigation of the physical sciences, he continued to maintain during the next two decades in which his major works were published. Gradually he accommodated his religious and scientific ideas to the main propositions of his philosophical pragmatism, as in *The Will to Believe* (1896) and *A Pluralistic Universe* (1909), but consistently with the freedom and tentativeness of his philosophical position generally, he did not force them into a systematic structure of beliefs. James's nearest approach to an ordered philosophy of religion was his Gifford Lectures of 1901 and 1902, published as *The Varieties of Religious Experience* (1902), in which he broke new ground for the psychology of religion by drawing his material from direct human experience of religious phenomena rather than from the hypothesis of physical or biological science or from the propositions of theology. For almost a generation thereafter, the influence of the *Varieties* tended to disintegrate systematic religious philosophy by emphasizing isolated religious experiences of an intense or unusual character rather than the unified religious experience of an integrated personality.

The recapture of human personality became, then, the starting point for James's analysis of the relationship between science and religion. It was the impersonality of science, he believed, which constituted its most serious defect. For among the presuppositions of science was the belief that the order of nature was exclusively mechanical, an explanation which was held to extend even to human life itself and which denied the force of personality as a condition of events.[1] But properly considered, James asserted, "the spirit and principles of science are mere affairs of method," and he believed that they implied nothing that need hinder science from "dealing successfully with a world in which personal forces are the starting-point of new effects."[2]

It was this sensitivity for the personal and subjective which compelled James to attack as false the distinctions which had hitherto been maintained between the method of science and that of the philosophical studies. From his point of view, the doctrine that the propositions of science were "reproductions" of an order of outer experience any more truly than were those of religion, ethics, or aesthetics could not be justified. All alike dealt with "ideal and universal relations amongst the objects of our thought." Their difference is one of degree, not of kind. It is to be found in the relative ease or difficulty with which nature's materials may be translated into scientific, aesthetic, or ethical forms. All are similarly relations among the objects of thought. Those relations which we call "scientific," however,

although they no more are inward *reproductions* of the outer order than the ethical and aesthetic relations are, yet they do not conflict with that order, but, once having sprung up by the play of the inward forces, are found—some of them at least, namely the only ones which have survived long enough to be matters of record— to be congruent with the time- and space-relations which our impressions affect.[3]

This concept of truth shifts the emphasis completely from a merely passive correspondence to a world of outer reality—the presupposition of the mechanists—to an active participation in it. The ethical truths of Christianity conflict with the outer world because they demand a transformation of the world to bring it into correspondence with a more essential truth than it possesses in its unredeemed state. But this is, indeed, the method of science itself, for science, too, transforms Nature as it brings outer experience into harmony with the ideal and universal relations of thought by means of which our comprehension of nature is achieved.

It was clear to James that the current tendency to refer science alone to the world of external nature rather than to that of mind was responsible for much of the confusion in the contemporary state of religion. For it followed that if all truth inhered somehow in external nature, then the truths of religion must also find their source and their validity in natural process. Indeed,

[1] William James, *The Will to Believe: And Other Essays in Popular Philosophy*, p. 324.
[2] *Ibid.*, p. 327.
[3] William James, *The Principles of Psychology* (2 vols.; New York, 1902), II, 639–40.

this was the position at which the generation of Draper, White, and Fiske, who sought in the doctrine of biological evolution the connection between science and religion, had now arrived. "The persons to whom I refer," James explained,

have still retained for the most part their nominal connection with Christianity, in spite of their discarding of its more pessimistic theological elements. But in that "theory of evolution" which, gathering momentum for a century, has within the past twenty-five years swept so rapidly over Europe and America, we see the ground laid for a new sort of religion of Nature, which has entirely displaced Christianity from the thought of a large part of our generation. The idea of a universal evolution lends itself to a doctrine of general meliorism and progress which fits the religious needs of the healthy-minded so well that it seems almost as if it might have been created for their use. Accordingly we find "evolutionism" interpreted thus optimistically and embraced as a substitute for the religion they were born in, by a multitude of our contemporaries who have either been trained scientifically, or been fond of reading popular science, and who had already begun to be inwardly dissatisfied with what seemed to them the harshness and irrationality of the orthodox Christian scheme.[4]

But the easy accommodation of spiritual meaning to the process of evolution was fast losing its hold upon a growing circle of men, among whom James mentioned himself. This natural religion, James asserted,

has suffered definitive bankruptcy [among persons] . . . who are growing more numerous every day. For such persons the physical order of nature, taken simply as science knows it, cannot be held to reveal any one harmonious spiritual intent.[5]

How, then, to explain the hold which natural religion had maintained over its adherents during the latter decades of the nineteenth century? The essential explanation in James's analysis is that natural religion permitted an indulgence of human ego which contradicted the claims upon selflessness perceived by Christian insights. This led to a religion of "healthy-mindedness" which proclaimed the natural goodness of man and denied the existence of evil. It began as an involuntary and immediate feeling of happiness, but proceeded quickly to a systematic assertion of the essential and universal goodness of all being, deliberately excluding evil from its field of vision. How easily such a view could be used for escaping responsibility for social evils was clear. James recognized that the systematic cultivation of healthy-mindedness was grounded in human nature itself. In spite of the fact that our professed theol-

[4] William James, *The Varieties of Religious Experience: A Study in Human Nature*, p. 90.
[5] *The Will to Believe*, p. 52.

ogy should forbid the indiscriminate attribution of goodness to all experience, nevertheless

We divert our attention from disease and death as much as we can; and the slaughter-houses and indecencies without end on which our life is founded are huddled out of sight and never mentioned, so that the world we recognize officially in literature and in society is a poetic fiction far handsomer and cleaner and better than the world that really is.[6]

The religion of healthy-mindedness, James pointed out, had been for the past fifty years substituted for Christianity even in the churches, where the advance of so-called "liberalism" had displaced the older theology. This view repudiated the conceptions of human depravity and eternal punishment and held instead that a consciousness of sin was symptomatic of the "sick soul" and therefore altogether "unnatural" and reprehensible.

It was clear to James that at the center of the problem of science and religion lay the question of human evil. The empirical fact of evil was there for the practitioners of the religion of healthy-mindedness as it was for everybody, but the practical point of view of their system prevented them from giving attention to it as a real problem. Thus the mind-curers forsook entirely the theology of ordinary Christians. They made use of traditional Christian terminology, but inverted the Christian hierarchy of sins:

whereas Christian theology has always considered *frowardness* to be the essential vice of this part [the "lower" part] of human nature, the mind-curers say that the mark of the beast in it is *fear*; and this is what gives such an entirely new religious turn to their persuasion.[7]

Thus the mind-curer, ignoring or underestimating the perversity of human nature, ranks as the source of greatest evil man's necessary anxiety as he views the hiatus between his moral achievements and the divine commands.

Thus James definitely rejected the claims of natural religion to find in the processes of Nature the source and justification for man's religious experiences. But he went much further than this, for he asserted positively that the realm of genuine religious experience transcended nature and was not to be reduced to terms of natural phenomena.

Religion has meant many things in human history; but when from now onward I use the word I mean to use it in the supernaturalist sense, as declaring that the so-called order of nature, which constitutes this world's experience, is only one portion of the total universe, and that there stretches beyond this visible world an un-

---

[6] *The Varieties of Religious Experience*, p. 89. [7] *Ibid.*, p. 96.

seen world of which we now know nothing positive, but in its relation to which the true significance of our present mundane life consists.[8]

Human experience was held to enter a dimension not measured by the criteria of natural science, to be contrasted to the "sensible and usually 'understandable' world." This region might indiscriminately be called "mystical" or "supernatural." Its distinguishing characteristic was that it was larger than ourselves, and that it was reached through man's moral striving. In this realm man's ideal impulses have their source, and man belongs to it in a more intimate sense even than he belongs to the sensible world, for, as James puts it, "we belong in the most intimate sense wherever our ideals belong." Man's real being, therefore, lies in the region from which he draws his spiritual strength, a region which James always sets in clear opposition to the natural order. In this fashion James declares his independence of the evolutionists and reasserts a doctrine of human personality which recognizes the depths of man's natural anxieties and the heights from which his moral insights take their origin.

Given James's insistence on the necessity of distinguishing between the realms of the natural and the supernatural, it followed that he would distinguish between science and religion as activities appropriate to these realms. Thus under James's analysis the relationship between science and religion tended to be broken. The scientist—even the scientist of religions—had no warrant for faith from his study of the phenomena of human experience, and less in the study of nature. However devout the scientist in his personal religious life, "the days are over," James felt, "when it could be said that for Science herself the heavens declare the glory of God and the firmament showeth his handiwork."[9] Indeed, in his moments of scientific activity, the scientist is so much a materialist that his findings tend to undermine the very foundations of religion. The scientist of religions himself uncovers in his investigations so many crimes and falsehoods masquerading as religious verities that a presumption against any religious belief easily arises in his mind. This explained, he thought, the current belief that religion was only an anachronism, a survival of a mode of thought which a more enlightened humanity had outgrown. It would seem that science, which repudiates both personality and purpose, constructing her theories "quite careless of their bearing on human anxieties and fates," must, then, repudiate religion.

How might this consequence be averted? By recognizing a plurality of "interpenetrating spheres of reality," each amenable to methods appropriate

[8] *The Will to Believe*, p. 51.   [9] *The Varieties of Religious Experience*, pp. 506–7.

to its nature and yielding profits characteristic of the purposes of the different men who handle it. Many systems of ideas, many different conceptions, many attitudes are applicable to the world in which we live, a world too complex and too proliferous to be exhausted by any partial or exclusive procedure. Nor could we ever devise a system so complete or of such wide applicability that it would reduce experience to terms of nature and reason. The human mind itself contains an element of perversity—James calls it a "twist"—which makes it impossible for any one type of mind to discern the totality of truth. The "scientific-academic" mind and the "feminine-mystical" mind fly from each other's temper and spirit.[10] And yet when the investigator pushes the claims of either science or religion to its ultimate presuppositions or conclusions, he finds that the most persistently held belief is not a matter of experience at all, but that "our conviction of its truth is far more like a religious faith than like assent to a demonstration."[11] Thus the plurality of worlds, which respond equally to the probings of science and to the entreaties of religion, are grounded ultimately in an act of faith.

The area for the reconciliation of science and religion, the basic presupposition from which both take their origin, James believed, was the reality of human personality. This is the fundamental fact which requires an act of faith for its affirmation. Thus James lies in the tradition of that Christian mysticism which took its inspiration from Augustine, for he emphasizes the transcendent reality of inner human experience. The essential reality of which man has his only immediate experience is his experience of himself. Every category of our thinking reduces ultimately to "one of the abstract elements" of the category of personality, which is the only complete category.[12] Science is accustomed to disregard this by pretending an impersonality of attitude in abstracting from human experience and proclaiming truths of a cosmic and general order, but these, James insists, are only the symbols of reality. But when, on the other hand, *we deal with private and personal phenomena as such, we deal with realities in the completest sense of the term.*[13] And dealing with the universe in this way is what James means by being religious. Man's only contact with ultimate reality is at the point of personal experience; his private destinies keep him in responsible relationship with the only absolute realities he can know.[14]

If the realities of human personality provided the nexus for science and religion, it followed for James that a science of religions should deal with the

---

[10] *The Will to Believe*, p. 301.   [11] *The Principles of Psychology*, II, 637.
[12] *The Will to Believe*, p. 327.   [13] *The Varieties of Religious Experience*, p. 489.
[14] *Ibid.*, p. 493.

data of personal religious experience. He believed that science could formulate from this data a body of essential doctrine common to religious experience to which physical science would not object. It was the duty of a science of religions, he thought, "to keep religion in connection with the rest of science,"[15] wherefore it must formulate from those articles of faith which have maintained themselves with increasing vitality through the vicissitudes of history a "reconciling hypothesis, and recommend it for general belief."[16] In the formulation of such general religious propositions, James felt that science had nothing to fear from the current fermentation in the religious world. And although the most satisfactory and enduring religious propositions would be those which incorporated the hypotheses of science, this did not mean that religion must surrender hypotheses of its own to which science had not given assent. Every scientist must allow, he insisted, that some religious hypothesis may be true, and not maintain that science had already "ruled all possible religious hyptheses out of court."[17]

The region of human personality, which provided an immediate experience of reality and furnished both science and religion with the data for their researches, also reaffirmed the existence of a transcendent world from whose perspective the insights of religion gained profounder meaning. Man does not rest satisfied with a mere charting and measurement of the natural world but demands the formulation of uniform laws through which he may better comprehend it. So also human needs outrun the visible universe, a fact which James advances to suggest that an invisible universe may be there. Science cannot debar man from trusting religious demands, since science is limited to a consideration of problems which involve sensible data.[18]

But if the invisible world is affirmed as a consequence of human needs, it derives also as a construct of human activity. "I confess," James wrote, "that I do not see why the very existence of an invisible world may not in part depend on the personal response which any one of us may make to the religious appeal."[19] He thought of human personality as creative, as participating with God through activity at the highest moral level possible to man in making the universe better. Thus the continued moral activity of man was a testimonial to the existence of a world that transcended nature, for only on the

---

[15] The Varieties of Religious Experience, p. 501.

[16] The Will to Believe, p. xii. James himself made a beginning in this direction when he reduced the fundamental elements in which all religions appear to meet to two: (1) an uneasiness, and (2) its solution. The uneasiness derives from a sense that there is "something wrong about us," and the solution presupposes a "proper connection with the higher powers" (The Varieties of Religious Experience, p. 498).

[17] The Will to Believe, p. xiii.   [18] Ibid., p. 56.   [19] Ibid., p. 61.

assumption that moral activity contributed in some real and permanent fashion to the eternal scheme of things could it have meaning.

James's strongest argument for the validity of the transcendent world, however, rests neither upon human need nor upon human morality. He makes the leap from the reality of intimate personal experience to that of the invisible world by means of the irreducible facts of tragedy and evil, which at once emphasize the poignancy of the human predicament and point beyond it to a realm where suffering is alleviated and evil reconciled. The doctrine that evil was instrumental to the greater perfection of the universe was repugnant to James because it seemed to invite toleration of an evil so great that it defied all human tolerance. The fact of evil contradicted all systematic doctrines of theological unity.[20] But religious men uniformly affirm a dimension in which the ideal order is permanently guaranteed, in which God reigns secure and overcomes all evil. Paradoxically, this affirmation is strengthened, not weakened, by the multiplication of evils in the world. The existence of tragedy continually emphasizes the need for a faith profound enough to transcend the crises of history, so that "where God is, tragedy is only provisional and partial, and shipwreck and dissolution are not the absolutely final things."[21] Such a hypothesis, because it predicts objective consequences of faith, is alone adequate to save religion from the subjectivism to which it is tempted from a reliance upon the data of personal experience. Thus James recognizes the paradox of the self and the other in religion: for, although the self is most clearly and authentically affirmed in the tragic history of the human personality, it is this sense of tragedy which points the self beyond itself for its fulfillment.

James's emphasis upon the personal element in religious experience was doubtless his outstanding contribution to the problem of the relationship of science and religion. Had it not been for the care with which he distinguished the somewhat pathological religious "experiences" from the character of religious experience generally, he might indeed have warranted the criticism of William Temple that he associated the religious life too easily with "moments of specially intense awareness."[22] But he sees clearly that the essential religious experience is that which finds the ground of its being in an order beyond and above the self, which is approached through the claims of the moral consciousness and through the moral life. A second element of sig-

---

[20] From a quotation in David Starr Jordan, *The Stability of Truth: A Discussion of Reality as Related to Thought and Action* (New York, 1911), pp. 68–69.

[21] *The Varieties of Religious Experience*, p. 507.

[22] William Temple, *Nature, Man and God* (New York, 1935), p. 334.

nificance in James's approach to the problem of the relationship of science and religion is his insistence that religious dogmas, like the doctrines of science, must find their justification in the practical consequences for good that they can effect in the contemporary world. This is a proposition consistent with the instrumental doctrines affirmed in his general pragmatic philosophy. But it was also an indictment of the bankruptcy of the late nineteenth-century Christianity which had surrendered to the determinisms of natural religion. That no concrete consequence should result in the universe from the fact of God's being there seemed to James an incredible proposition. The world interpreted religiously must in actual fact be a different world in its natural constitution from the world posited by materialistic science.

It is strange, I have heard a friend say [James wrote], to see this blind corner into which Christian thought has worked itself at last, with its God who can raise no particular weight whatever, who can help us with no private burden, and who is on the side of our enemies as much as he is on our own.[23]

It was true that, in its haste to embrace the apostles of the new science, the religious thought of the 1890's had destroyed the moral character of the universe. That this was not so much the fault of science as of social philosophy and of religion James was quick to see. He repudiated the "universalistic supernaturalism" which he held had surrendered to the current materialism by taking the facts of physical science at their face value, and leaving "the laws of life just as naturalism finds them, with no hope of remedy, in case their fruits are bad."[24] But he did not withhold his criticism from the scientists, whose pretensions persuaded them that their findings were complete and final. "Our science is a drop," he wrote, "our ignorance a sea." The world of natural knowledge, he held, lay within the larger and more valid world of ideals, which were grasped more accurately through religious conduct and religious feelings than through theories, whether religious or scientific. The real world, according to James, was certainly not the world confined within "the narrow 'scientific' bounds."[25] The world of personal experience, which was also the world which transcends personal experience, was for James a world so wondrously and intricately built that it defied alike the attempts of scientific pretension and of religious dogma to exhaust it. But it responded to the participation of human personalities, aware of their responsibilities for moral action, because it was a world in which the moral life had meaning and permanence far greater than natural religion could validate.

[23] *The Varieties of Religious Experience*, p. 512 n.
[24] *Ibid.*, p. 511.   [25] *Ibid.*, p. 509.

5

The Democratic Synthesis
David Starr Jordan

DAVID STARR JORDAN, successively president, chancellor, and chancellor emeritus of Stanford University over a period of more than forty years, shared many of James's insights into the problem of the relationship of science and religion. Jordan considered himself a pragmatist, and if not a follower of James at least a co-originator along with him of the philosophic point of view which best expressed the interests and the attitudes of the scientist. Both were laboratory scientists. Jordan was primarily interested in extending and systematizing the knowledge of fishes as James had organized and deepened man's knowledge of his own behavior. The concrete fact had for both Jordan and James a compelling attraction. Both were chary of generalizations and sought the profounder meanings of human experience in particular data. But Jordan, unlike James, had been deeply touched by the struggle of science and the church as seen by Draper, and later by White's account of the conflict of science and theology. Throughout his life he referred to these works with approval. As a consequence, Jordan's writings were much more sensitive to the struggle between science and religion than were those of any other figure in the controversy during his generation. Indeed, his life and writings comprehend almost exactly the period of inquiry into the relationship of science and religion from the impact of Darwinism in the 1870's to the controversy over the teaching of evolution in the schools in the 1920's. From Jordan's first publication on this subject, an article on "The Church and Modern Thought" in 1891, to his last book, *The Higher Foolishness* (1927), he gave attention to the nature of the conflict between science and religion and to the possibilities for their reconciliation. In addition, his private correspondence during the decade of the 1920's repeated the more formally stated findings of his published books and articles.

In this long record of publication and correspondence, Jordan tempered considerably the extravagant indictments returned against religion by Andrew D. White. Although he identified himself throughout his life with the army of science for whom White had fashioned the standard, he yet maintained a sensitivity to religious needs and a respect for religious motives. The

object of his attack was never religion itself, but rather religion corrupted by
ignorance, superstition, or tradition. He undertook to distinguish legitimate
religion, which he understood in the sense of Matthew Arnold as "the power
that makes for righteousness," from the mere externals of religion, which
were too easily corrupted into empty dogmas or ceremonies. But most of
Jordan's consideration of the problem of the relationship of science and religion was fragmentary, for Jordan was not a systematic thinker outside the
field of his scientific competence. His nearest approach to a finished and
organized treatise on a philosophic subject was his John Calvin McNair lectures at the University of North Carolina in 1910, published under the title
of *The Stability of Truth* in 1911.

Although Jordan was tireless as a publicist in the interest of science, his
works do not exhibit the steady growth in insight into the religious problem
which sometimes characterizes the thought of one whose major interest is
speculative or whose training and discipline have come from dialectics. Jordan's contribution to the discussion of the relationship of science and religion
is therefore limited to a reiteration through the years with minor variations
of a few leading propositions which he formulated early in his career and
held steadfastly throughout his life. But if there is little originality or growth
in his thought, it is nevertheless characterized by an attitude of moderation
and tentativeness which distinguishes it clearly from the utterances of many
scientists of his generation. For his writings were distinguished throughout
by a sense of justice which raises them far above the general level of his period,
and by a common-sense wisdom which testifies to his universality of interest
and ease of comprehension in a field remote from his specialized training.
The truly surprising thing about Jordan's long record of discussion regarding
the relationship of science and religion is that, in a period when secular presuppositions were dominant in American life, he should have achieved such
a high level of insight into the nature and problems not only of science but
of religion as well.

In the decade of the 1890's he entered the controversy over science and
religion with an article in the *Overland Monthly* in October 1891, an allegory
of man's moral pilgrimage published in 1896 under the title *The Innumerable
Company*, and an address at a meeting of the Unitarian Club of California
in San Francisco on April 26, 1897. In these early writings, he presented several of the leading propositions which he was to emphasize again and again
in his later works and his correspondence. Among them was the suggestion
that, since absolute truth was impossible to science and all knowledge was
necessarily tentative, the reconciliation of science and religion could be ac-

complished in circumstances of the completest freedom of thought and expression. Holding that each man must find for himself the most adequate road to moral salvation and must not impose his way upon others, he applied this proposal to the moral situation as well as to the quest for truth. He also held, as he was to repeat many times in his later writings, that the essential struggle of science and religion was a psychological struggle which originated in the human mind and was projected from there into society and history.

The basis for the struggle, as Jordan analyzed it in "The Church and Modern Thought," was to be found in the opposition of a priori knowledge and inductive knowledge, but this was merely a reduction to logical terms of a contest between the opposing parties which represented these contrasting methods of inquiry. Whereas the scientist relied upon induction from experience, the "church dominant" deduced its dogma from its corpus of sacred writings with no regard for the facts of ordinary life. But Jordan, unlike Draper, did not hold the church alone responsible for the warfare against modern science. The conflict was a necessary one wherever a priori thinking held sway, and especially when an organized body of men, of which the church indeed was a good illustration, undertook to make any body of truth its exclusive property and responsibility. For truth, even scientific truth, being tentative and imperfect because derived from data necessarily incomplete and fragmentary, had a way of eluding the grasp of any power that sought to control and monopolize it. All truth contained an ingredient of error which, if left uncorrected, ultimately corrupted the truth that contained it, especially if that truth was promulgated as dogma by a body of men claiming power. And yet Jordan could not completely discard the conception of an unchanging truth in which the thinking of such social evolutionists as Fiske had been cast. At this stage he believed that science was coming constantly nearer to the idea of immutable law, as a substitute for the view that the world is governed by divine whim or by mere chance.[1]

If the antagonism of religion and science was really that of organized groups of men committed to different methods of arriving at truth, then it seemed to Jordan that the conflict could be resolved by permitting open competition between truth and error.

There is no way of preserving truth so effective as to give it an open field with error. When the breezes blow, the chaff flies. When a barrier shuts off the wind from the grain, the wheat is never winnowed.[2]

[1] David Starr Jordan, "The Church and Modern Thought," *Overland Monthly*, October 1891, p. 392. [2] *Ibid.*, p. 394.

And in such an atmosphere of freedom, he believed, there would arise a new kind of church, one not committed to opposing modern thought or even to guarding all knowable truth, but one that would stand at the center of scientific inquiry as a voluntary association of men and women to whom all truth is sacred.[3]

In *The Innumerable Company* Jordan described in allegorical form the journey of successive generations up the rocky mountainside of life to the distant river whose banks were shrouded in impenetrable mists. Many had made the journey, leaving maps and charts to mark the way they felt they could recommend to others. The most successful journey had been made by One who left a Chart on which those who had come afterwards had inscribed their own additions and interpretations, but none had succeeded in making the journey easier or the route more direct. With the passage of time, he felt, men had concluded that "the ways which are safe are innumerable as the multitude of those that may walk therein." Moreover, men had come to hold the old Chart in ever increasing reverence, realizing that its simple words contained profounder truth than the accumulation of glosses, and that no one should insist that meanings which he had found helpful should be made a law for others.[4] In this fashion Jordan early applied his view of the tentativity of truth to the problems of moral conduct and religious dogma.

But the conflict of religion and science involved much more, according to Jordan, than the formulation of truth or the direction of human conduct. It was applicable to social growth as well as to the development of the individual and governed the growth of civilization itself. This view he presented at the thirtieth meeting of the Unitarian Club of California on April 26, 1897, in an address entitled "The Conflict of Science." He discerned a clear progression from "seeing true" through "thinking right" and "right action" to "higher civilization." In this sequence Jordan believed that science was the guiding force.

"The world as it is," is the province of science. "The God of the things as they are," is the God of the highest heaven. As "the world as it is" to the sane man is glorious, beautiful, noble, and divine, so will science be the inspiration of art, poetry, and religion.[5]

Therefore, he concluded, science must be liberated and encouraged if civilization is to prosper.

[3] Jordan, "The Church and Modern Thought," *Overland Monthly*, October 1891, p. 395.

[4] Jordan, *The Innumerable Company* (Boston, 1896), no pagination.

[5] Jordan, "The Conflict of Science," in Unitarian Club of California, *Addresses at the Thirtieth Meeting* (San Francisco, [1897]), pp. 26–27.

The conflict of science, Jordan noted, had been variously described, some-times as a contest with prejudice and tradition, at other times as a conflict between dogmatism and knowledge, frequently also as a war against organized forces in society itself. But these he believed were derived from a more basic conflict still. He conceded that Draper had identified a part of the conflict in calling it a conflict with religion, and that White, too, had presented partial truth in defining it as a struggle with "Dogmatic Theology." But the essential struggle, Jordan felt, was more than these. It was

a conflict of tendencies in the human mind which has worked itself out into history. For all history is written in the human mind before it is brought to light on the great stage of the world.[6]

This view was one of his most frequently reiterated positions, and he recurred to it whenever he undertook to analyze the problem of the relationship of science and religion.

The tendencies in man's thinking which, projected into history, have become the conflict of science and religion are very difficult to eradicate, Jordan believed. Men cling to their religious notions with special persistence because they are so closely associated with moral conceptions and with the motives of conduct. But "much of what we call our religion to-day is simply the debris of our grandfathers' science." These notions form the mental universe in which we live, and from which we cannot escape without struggle and the ultimate destruction of much of our intellectual environment. Theological notions become entangled easily with ideas about science and morals. And since theology has been considered of greater importance than other disciplines for determining man's fate, theological conceptions have often dominated all other ideas. Therefore religious bodies have become strongholds of conservatism dedicated to the defense of outworn dogmas, and against them the experience of a single human life is too limited to achieve the necessary corrections which science and truth require.[7]

So the conflict, although it originates in the human mind, is fought out in society, and the survival of civilization is at stake in the struggle. The opposition of dogma and knowledge becomes finally a struggle to inhibit social development in the interest of conservatism or to stimulate society to action in the interest of progress:

Just as science goes over into action, so does dogmatism pass over into suppression. The struggle for democracy, the rise of the common man, is therefore part of the same great conflict for human freedom.[8]

Thus the conflict which begins in the human mind and later involves organ-

6 *Ibid.*, p. 21.   7 *Ibid.*, p. 28.   8 *Ibid.*, p. 29.

ized bodies of men fighting over articles of belief, becomes finally a social struggle between freedom and democracy, on the one hand, and oppression and political reaction, on the other.

Jordan's writings on the problem of the relationship of science and religion during the first decade of the twentieth century began with a note of doubt and ended strongly on a note of affirmation. Five small volumes were the product of this period, the last of which, *The Religion of a Sensible American*, dedicated to the memory of a Stanford professor of biology, was his nearest approach to a treatise on a religious problem. These years saw some development of Jordan's religious thinking. At the start he repeated the position familiar to naturalism that the workings of natural law assured the reconciliation of science and religion. But soon he emphasized the importance of religion for practical life and he finally endorsed pragmatism as the point of view that makes religion most meaningful.

In two little books, published in 1901 and 1902, Jordan developed two complementary aspects of scientific knowledge to which he had alluded in earlier writings. On the one hand, scientific knowledge was absolute knowledge in that it revealed the inexorable working of law in Nature. But the contrary view, that science gave only proximate answers limited by human experience, was the position that he emphasized more strongly. From the former point of view, the problem of evil seemed to Jordan unanswerable as a philosophical problem but susceptible of adequate explanation by science. From the analogies of biological evolution evil could be understood, he thought, as "uncompleted good . . . lack of adaptation in human affairs, failure in structure, or failure in intent . . ."[9] Evil actions in men rendered them less well adapted for survival and were modified or eliminated by the same mechanisms which brought about the alteration of species. This view is a complete capitulation to the rule of natural law in the province of human morality, and Jordan accepted it fully. For

a law of ethics is no more sacred, no more or less invariable than the law of rain. A law of nature is the expression of the wisest, the best, the only way of doing things. Such a law was never broken, can never be broken; for nothing in the universe will ever be done in an inferior way.[10]

In Jordan's analysis of the application of natural law to the problem of evil, there was at first a suggestion that he made a distinction between man and nature, affirming that nature was amoral and that the moral problem

[9] Jordan, *Standeth God Within the Shadow* (New York, 1901), p. 3.
[10] *Ibid.*, pp. 11–12.

applied only to man. "For nature neither loves nor hates," he held. "She is neither good nor cruel. She is merely the truth of God,—the God of 'the things as they are . . .' It is within ourselves and our relations that the good and evil find their place . . ."[11] But he did not long maintain this distinction. Although nature "makes no move toward goodness" and man alone has the capacity to revolt from cruelty and turn to love, Jordan maintained that even these human reactions, however complex they may appear, are nevertheless as equally under the control of natural laws as physics or chemistry. But there is yet a difference. For whereas an earlier representative of naturalism, such as John William Draper, could draw from the reign of natural law the conclusion of man's insignificance and impotence, Jordan affirmed instead man's freedom and power. His conclusion was optimistic, not pessimistic. The application of natural law to the human reaction assured the triumph of good over evil, which guaranteed, of course, the ascendency of science in its conflict with religion. Thus,

By the law of the human reaction, cruelty gives place to love, intolerance and bigotry to sweetness and light, the sword to the dynamo, and dogma to science.[12]

And this was not to be considered an undesirable outcome. This view, however, supported a position which he soon abandoned. It emphasized the absoluteness of scientific law, whereas Jordan returned again and again to the complementary aspect of science, its tentativeness and partiality because it was necessarily affected with human error.

That science of a body of proximate rather than ultimate answers to man's questions about the universe was Jordan's theme in a book entitled *The Philosophy of Despair*, which he published in 1902. The book was an answer, from the standpoint of the scientist, to certain stanzas of Edward FitzGerald's translation of Omar Khayyám's *Rubáiyát*, wherein the Persian poet had given expression to the sadness and the grandeur of insoluble problems. But instead of reaffirming the ability of science to dispel a pessimistic philosophy, Jordan emphasized the limitations of science and, at the same time, urged his readers not to seek unattainable absolutes whether through the methods of science or through the insights of any other disciplines.

In the presence of the infinite problem of life [he maintained], the voice of Science is dumb, for Science is the coördinate and corrected expression of human experience, and human experience must stop with the limitations of human life.[13]

Eschew absolutes, he counseled, for man cannot arrive at them however hard

[11] *Ibid.,*p. 15.   [12] *Ibid.,* p. 17.
[13] Jordan, *The Philosophy of Despair* (San Francisco, 1902), p. 10.

he tries. All knowledge is tentative because it rests on human experience and is affected by all the limitations, such as those which qualify sense perception, with which human personality is encompassed. Nor is there any appeal from experience to reason, for reason, being a "mere 'by-product in the process of Evolution,'" is but an instrument for systematizing sense perceptions and is itself conditioned by the accuracy of the sense perceptions with which it deals. Even the very complexity of life invalidates ultimates, for the most complicated instruments, however admirably fitted to highly specialized purposes, are thereby the most easily thrown out of adjustment, so that complexity not only provides no guaranty of stability but renders the instrument more completely dependent upon the environment to which it is related. But perhaps the most serious argument against the search for absolutes is that it inhibits action. For "To grasp at ultimate truth," says Jordan, "is to be forever empty-handed. To reach for the ultimate end of action is never to begin to act."[14]

So far, his analysis gave little in the way of an affirmative answer to the philosophy of despair. He did, however, despite the insecurity of all scientific truth, find some elements of hope. For one thing, evolution by looking always toward the future emphasized man's capacity for development. Man was potentially free in that he could look forward to the control of his environment and, therefore, to a more complete expression of his will. And with this increased freedom, Jordan believed, man would also achieve a sense of status in the Universe, based on the conviction

that the heart of the Universe is sound, that though there be so many of us in the world, each must have his place, and each at last "be somehow needful to infinity."[15]

Although science promised no absolutes, it did offer the highest attainable truth. But truth alone was not to be considered the end of science, for science implied virtue, and virtue, in its turn, promised higher levels of civilization. His answer to the philosophy of despair was, therefore, to encourage man to be satisfied with proximate truth, to embrace that "Fanaticism for Veracity" which was the proper attitude of science, and to leave ultimate truths to God.[16] The positive element was his insistence upon the release of human vitalities for action in the world, a position later to occupy a large place in Jordan's pragmatism.

It was not surprising, therefore, that as he looked forward to the religious possibilities of the future, he should predict that religion must play a larger

[14] *The Philosophy of Despair*, p. 18.   [15] *Ibid.*, p. 21.   [16] *Ibid.*, p. 33.

part in the affairs of practical life. In 1903 he published *The Call of the Twentieth Century*, written for men of college age as an answer to the charge that religion was not as important as heretofore in the complexities of modern life. Religion is not losing its hold, he said, it is simply changing its grip. The religion of the new century will be more practical and more real. It will break through its traditional confinement to the church and the Sabbath and affect every avenue of life every day of the week. Jordan affirmed that the spiritual leaders of the twentieth century would indeed be religious men. But he rejected as legitimate forms of religious activity the withdrawal of mystics, the doctrinal debates of schoolmen, and the liturgical exercises of formalists. Instead, he emphasized,

Their religion of the Twentieth Century will be its working theory of life. It will be expressed in simple terms or it may not be expressed at all, but it will be deep graven in the heart. In wise and helpful life it will find ample justification. It will deal with the world as it is in the service of "the God of things as they are."[17]

Such a religion, he thought, would relate to the world as it really was, not as a vale of tears or as a place of sin, but as "a working paradise in which the rewards of right doing are instant and constant." Thus, in Jordan's view, men's religious capacities become creative not merely in the movement from discussion to action but in action itself whenever it is immediately relevant to the problems of life.

Granted that a practical religion requires men to engage actively in the work of the world, could it not be argued that all of men's energies are necessary to achieve his survival in the struggle of life, leaving nothing extra to devote to common concerns? Jordan formulated his answer to this question in 1908 in *The Higher Sacrifice*. He held that the exceptional man had something over and above the requirements of life to give to his fellows. On such men has the progress of civilization depended:

It is the strong, wise, and good of the past who have made our lives possible. It is the great human men, the "men in the natural order," that have made it possible for "the plain, common men" that make up civilization to live, rather than merely to vegetate.[18]

Such men ask from society no rewards for their contributions. It is according to "the natural order of things," he believed, that they live above all considerations of pay or glory. The universities are dedicated to the training of

---

[17] Jordan, *The Call of the Twentieth Century, an Address to Young Men* (Boston, 1903), p. 73.

[18] Jordan, *The Higher Sacrifice* (Boston, 1908), p. 47.

these men and call upon them for the "higher sacrifice" of their exceptional gifts to the common good. And such a demand could be properly made because these gifts, like the sunshine, came from God. Because they proceeded from a common source, spiritual leadership and scientific discovery could not come into conflict. The researches of a Helmholtz, no less than the spiritual insights of a Shakespeare, were, in Jordan's opinion, gifts beyond the needs of survival flowing "from the same inexhaustible divine reservoir."[19]

Near the end of the decade Jordan summarized the views of "a sensible American" on religion and its relationship to science in an article written for the *Hibbert Journal* and later expanded and published separately as a book. The sensible American was Wilbur Wilson Thoburn, a professor of bionomics at Stanford University who had died in 1899. Jordan set down Thoburn's views from memory, with his own endorsement, from notes and unpublished fragments which Thoburn had written. This small treatise was Jordan's nearest approach to an analysis of the meaning and purpose of religion. In it he explained how the demand that religion apply to the problems of life would affect the attitudes of the ordinary man, and how the apparent conflict of science and religion would dissolve before the pragmatism of the sensible American.

The religion of the sensible American, he wrote, was a religion of life, of activity. He held that faith, truth, and doctrine all involved elements of activity, and that only in activity did their essential meaning appear. The key to heaven was faith in self, but such faith was not given; it was the result of experience and had to be won by constant exercise. Likewise, truth was no empty system of principles but was an instrument for service, so that religion, according to Jordan, "finds its function and justification in the conduct of life."[20] And so far as doctrine was concerned, it was true, he thought, that a man must know what he believes, but "no truth is ours until we first live it, until it enters into our lives and we become it."[21] The simplest statement of doctrine, therefore, seemed enough to define man's relationship to the universe.

The single word, *Credo, I believe* [italics *sic*], is surely adequate. It implies faith in the universe, in man, and in all the forces inside or outside ourselves which shall make for righteousness.[22]

This approach to religious ideas was clearly pragmatic, and now for the first

---

[19] *The Higher Sacrifice*, p. 44.
[20] Jordan, "The Religion of the Sensible American," *Living Age*, July 25, 1908, p. 197 (reprinted from the *Hibbert Journal*). Although the views related are attributed to Thoburn, they are assumed to be also those of Jordan.
[21] *Ibid.*, p. 199.   [22] *Ibid.*, pp. 197–98.

time he acknowledged the philosophical kinship of his views on religion. Pragmatism, said Jordan, is the position that whatever will work in the conduct of life has elements of truth in it. He recognized very clearly, however, how difficult it was to distinguish between these elements of truth and elements of error which are also always present. The fact that religion "works" to the extent of providing charity and furnishing consolation in time of trouble "proves," he said, that there is truth in it. But it does not by any means prove that all religion is true, or that the founders of any particular religion were animated by truth or virtue. In this ambiguous predicament, it therefore becomes the business of science and of philosophy—which, according to Jordan, is the logic of science—to separate from the errors of religion those elements on which the conduct of life may safely rest.[23]

However important he thought the task of distinguishing the valid from the erroneous elements in religion, he did not underestimate its difficulties or its dangers. For it was indeed possible that such an enterprise would merely accentuate the apparent antagonism between science and religion rather than resolve it. In the dilemma which confronted the modern intellectual, science and religion appeared to be in conflict when, from Jordan's point of view, the real issue was between the tendency to identify religion with its institutional forms and its dogmas and the teaching that progress is possible only by opposing institutions and by rejecting the dogmas associated with them. Out of this impasse the religious man seemed to have only two alternatives, he argued, and neither alternative was an acceptable one. The first course was the familiar device of separating the religious life from the intellectual life, with consequences very disturbing, he thought, to the former. Even more dangerous was the second alternative, which tempted the believer to distrust reason and deny experience so far as they led him away from his faith. This point of view systematically denies that anything is real and affirms that therefore even disease, deformation, and sin are nonexistent. The sensible American, Jordan asserted, rightly recognized and rejected the essential selfishness implicit in the serenity cultivated by representatives of this position. The proper response to the discovery that life was set about with obstacles and tragic impediments was not to deny their reality but rather to affirm man's power to transcend them.

What we need for effective life [Jordan wrote] is more faith in our environment, not less. More faith in reality of matter and force and more faith in the power of the human soul to stand above it.[24]

[23] Jordan, *The Religion of a Sensible American* (Boston, 1909), p. 57.
[24] *Ibid.*, p. 70.

No subjectivist metaphysics could provide any adequate basis for distinguishing between the creative elements in religion and the mass of outworn ideas with which they were associated.

But, when properly considered, this apparent antagonism between science and religion is found by Jordan to be itself unreal. There is indeed, he says, a constant struggle "between new ideas and preconceived ideas, between discovery and tradition," but this is not a conflict of religion, defined as the impulse to strive for the highest and best in human conduct, and science, which is the means for determining which particular ideals are highest and which actions best. And even the struggle between new conceptions and traditional ones, which necessarily involves individual men and the history of human society, is bound to reach a favorable outcome. The truth is sure to survive in the long run, Jordan predicted, and meanwhile "the wisdom of the race" is never in conflict with the worthiest ideals, which guide men to life's most repaying experiences.[25] Therefore the sensible American can recognize no antagonism between science and religion, between the words of Jesus and the teachings of human experience tested and set in order.

The religion of the sensible American is, therefore, not one of creed or ceremony or emotion, not one primarily of the intellect, but a religion of faith and love and action—a confidence that the universe of matter and of spirit is a reality, that its functions are in wise hands, for the time being our own hands as well as the hand of God, and our part is to help our brother organisms to more abounding life.[26]

Thus Jordan concluded his writings on the problem of science and religion during the first decade of the twentieth century with a note of optimism. He emphasized propositions familiar and congenial to the American of the progressive era—that life is real, that man is free and wise as he participates with God in the management of the universe, and that his mission is to contribute more abundantly to the enhancement of life.

The optimism of the progressive period was rudely shattered by the events of the second decade of the century, which saw the United States turn from a major interest in domestic reform to a position of leadership in international politics. During these years Jordan's principal extracurricular interest was his participation in the movement for world peace, but he found occasion nevertheless to give attention to the problem of science and religion. In the John Calvin McNair lectures at the University of North Carolina, published in 1911 as *The Stability of Truth*, he restated in somewhat more sys-

[25] *The Religion of a Sensible American*, p. 20.
[26] "The Religion of the Sensible American," *Living Age*, July 25, 1908, p. 204.

tematic fashion some of his earlier notions regarding the conflict of scientific and religious thought and hinted at a modification of pragmatism toward a greater relevance to life. This question was to receive greater attention in Jordan's correspondence and unpublished fragments in the following decade. After the United States had entered the first World War, Jordan went into print again to challenge the scientific accuracy of the "social Darwinism" which held that war was a necessary step in the evolution of society. These works contributed little that was new to the discussion, but they served to emphasize further Jordan's view that scientific knowledge, although tentative, provided an adequate basis for the conduct of life and an adequate inspiration for the cultural niceties of civilization.

A dozen years after the publication of *The Stability of Truth* Jordan stated that he had written it "as a reply to Haeckel's misuse of Monism, as a basis on which biological deductions . . . could be predicated."[27] He proposed, instead, that truth was stable, not because all life could be reduced to forms of matter, but because in the course of history the findings of men of science, although they seemed to represent the weaker side, would ultimately win out over the "dominant forces of society." In other words, the stability of truth was itself at stake in the conflict between science and religion, but a favorable issue was assured because the side of science had "the strength of the universe behind" it.[28]

How could Jordan be so sure of this optimistic outcome? For a part of his answer he recurred to the old proposition that the evolutionary process selects for survival "those lines of conduct which make for life and strength" and which are endorsed as "righteousness" by the religions of the world.[29] Thus it seemed clear to Jordan that history had achieved the subordination of the lower to the higher motives in life, and that this achievement was

the certain trend of human evolution, as it has been the ideal of those who, in the name of religion, have striven worthily for man's spiritual advancement.[30]

But Jordan did not have to depend only on the doctrine of evolution to prove that the activities of men of science, and with them the common experiences of mankind generally, were valid. A substantial rebuttal to the philosophy of despair was the discovery from experience that pessimism was not

[27] David Starr Jordan to Scudder Klyce, December 18, 1923, Jordan Correspondence, Vol. LXXXIII.

[28] Jordan, *The Stability of Truth, a Discussion of Reality as Related to Thought and Action*, pp. 170–71.

[29] *Ibid.*, p. 24.

[30] *Ibid.*, p. 63.

livable. Jordan now suggested that the pragmatic test of "workableness" give way to the more general test of "livableness." Although labels never accurately define a thinker's precise turns of thought, Jordan's position may at this point be better described as "vitalism" than as "pragmatism." He now developed a suggestion from one of his earlier writings proposing that the conflict between science and religion would disappear at the level of involvement in life. The pragmatic doctrine of workableness would reconcile religion and science by restricting the area of inquiry to the conditions of the particular problem at issue, judging the validity of a religious proposition by the consequences of holding it. But Jordan would widen the area of inquiry to the whole of life, asserting that the truth of a proposition is to be judged by whether one is willing to trust his life to it. Thus the alternative to pessimism is held to be not a denial of the reality of life's hazards but an assertion of life's meaningfulness accompanied by an active participation in its work. To believe that life is worth living, to trust in external reality, to engage actively in life, and to be happy—these, said Jordan, are the ingredients of the abundant life, and what is more, all are "justified by the tests of science."[31] They are the essential elements of religion because they are unchanging elements, and because experience has shown that mankind may safely rely upon them to develop the highest values of civilization.

. . . the verities of human life, the common experience of love, sorrow, hope, faith, action, religion [said Jordan], these do not change. Like the truths of external nature, all these are forever renewed and verified by renewed human experience. Love makes for life. Action is life. To give life more abundantly, is the essence of religion. We can trust life, that life is worth living. We can trust action; for action is the primal purpose of feeling and thinking. We can trust love, for it has its justification in happy and wholesome life. These intangible forces, on which rests the development of religion, have been pre-eminently safe in the history of mankind.[32]

To Jordan it seemed eminently clear that a vitalist philosophy was justified by the findings of science. Might it not also be possible to find scientific justification for a system of morals? To this problem Jordan now turned.

Jordan believed that science was the source of ethics as of truth about the physical universe. Science taught that men should live here and now in mutual love and helpfulness. This ideal, said Jordan,

has been in constant antithesis to the ethics of ecclesiasticism, of asceticism, and of militarism, as well as to the fancies of the various groups of "intellectual malcontents to whom the progress of science seems slow and laborious."[33]

[31] *The Stability of Truth*, p. 51.   [32] *Ibid.*, p. 44.   [33] *Ibid.*, p. 171.

The scientific ideal is altruism. And why? Because science itself "is the flower of human altruism."[34] No worker in science can stand alone, Jordan asserted, nor does any scientist who tries to do so make a significant contribution. Every scientist must enter into the work of others and fit his thought to theirs. Every scientist is indebted beyond hope of payment to the past for the accumulation of data with which he begins, and his own experiences do not belong to himself alone but are part of the heritage of the future. In his article on "Social Darwinism" Jordan carried the argument a step further. Arguing against the proposition that frightfulness and barbarism are the qualities precipitated by the struggle for existence, he maintained, on the contrary, that altruism rather than selfishness had the greater survival value. Altruism, said Jordan, is an impulse as deeply planted in human nature as hunger and as difficult to eradicate. It requires no artificial means of preservation, for individuals who are wanting in altruism die without descendants. "There is a bounty on their heads," Jordan argued, "whether they be wolves, or hawks, or predatory men."[35] Thus altruism survives in the struggle for existence while barbarism perishes. And altruism as a moral philosophy wins further approval of science because its survival can be explained by reference to the doctrine of evolution, a theory which itself has achieved scientific validation.

Jordan's analysis of the grounds for conflict between science and religion in *The Stability of Truth* was little more than a repetition of views already expressed. But they were now accompanied by the stronger emphasis upon activity and novelty with which his formulation of the philosophy of abundant living had been stated. Again he insisted that the conflict was essentially a psychological one between tendencies in the human mind which later worked themselves out in history. The conflict sometimes took the form of new ideas opposed to the notions of childhood, which we held with special persistence because they were associated with conceptions of right and wrong. The scientist, Jordan felt, was so often a party to the contest with religion because his function was the discovery of new truth, which by its very unfamiliarity and by its contrast with popular fictions aroused the opposition of the multitude. It was the business of the scientist to oppose his "facts," which in Jordan's mind were equivalent to objective reality, to the traditional and outworn notions of science held by the average man. But still the most important element in the conflict, as Jordan saw it, was the social pressure which supported error and against which the truths of science had to make their way as best they could. In this contest the Church frequently became the organizer of con-

[34] *Ibid.*, pp. 172–73.
[35] Jordan, "Social Darwinism," *The Public*, March 30, 1918, p. 401.

servatism because it possessed a body of theological dogma which touched all departments of knowledge and which made a more powerful claim for men's loyalties than the mere facts of science. Thus the body of theological opinion guarded by the Church became a nucleus for organization, around which the conservative elements in society could gather to wage war upon the separated bands of science.[36] From this analysis of the struggle between science and religion, Jordan concluded that its essential element was the effort of the human mind to grasp reality and to relate itself to nature, a process which required the repudiation of philosophy and history alike. The real struggle, said Jordan,

is the effort of the human mind to relate itself to realities in the midst of traditions and superstitions, to realize that Nature never contradicts herself, is always complex, but never mysterious. As a final result all past systems of philosophy, if not all possible systems, have been thrown back into the realm of literature, of poetry. They can no longer dogmatically control the life of action, each forward step of which must take its departure from present aim and present fact. In the warfare of tradition against science the real and timely in act and motive has striven to replace the unreal and the obsolete.[37]

Such a reliance upon activity and novelty took Jordan a step nearer to a philosophy of anti-intellectualism. His movement from pragmatism to vitalism had been a step in the same direction. And yet it is difficult to take what would appear to be a repudiation of literature and poetry as guides for human life too seriously when one recalls Jordan's continuing interest in all the arts of civilized living and his prediction that the twentieth century would behold

a great increase of precision in each branch of human knowledge, a great widening of the horizon of human thought, [and] a great improvement in the conditions of human life, as enlightened purpose, intelligence, and precision rise to be more and more controlling factors in human action.[38]

At the same time, Jordan was well aware of the extent to which the findings of science could be perverted to special purposes. In the doctrines of "Social Darwinism," developed in Germany in the half-century just past, he could see how the theory of evolution had been turned to support an existing dynastic system, and he did his best to point out its errors and dangers.[39] But it might also have occurred to him that his own pragmatist and vitalist doctrines

---

[36] *The Stability of Truth*, p. 169.

[37] *Ibid.*, p. 171.

[38] *Ibid.*, p. 175.

[39] "Social Darwinism," *The Public*, March 30, 1918, p. 400.

were susceptible of the same use, for they might not always be asserted with the same tentativity and humaneness which characterized his formulation of them.

The years between the end of the first World War and the depression of 1929 were crucial for the conflict between science and religion. The decade of the 1920's began on a note of optimism and confidence as the leaders of the victorious allies looked to the scientific accomplishment which had won the war to bring about a secure prosperity. In the course of the decade, American men of science frequently made pronouncements asserting the sufficiency of scientific knowledge as a basis for religious doctrines. That the views of the scientists, however, were not universally held by the average American became increasingly apparent as the popular movement to control the teaching of evolution in the schools reached its dramatic climax in the trial of John Thomas Scopes at Dayton, Tennessee, and involved such notable antagonists as Clarence Darrow and William Jennings Bryan. It is not surprising that Jordan should have been active in publicizing the issue of the conflict of science and religion during these years, and there came from his pen a half-dozen articles, a small booklet, and, under the title of *The Higher Foolishness*, a collection of essays, some of them previously published. In these writings Jordan did not make for science the extravagant claims which so often characterized the work of his colleagues in science. On the contrary, his response to the controversy of the 1920's was a more profound respect for the claims of religion and an effort to defend it against the secular criticism of the age.

Jordan was by now convinced that religion, properly understood, should be involved in no conflict with science. The conflict was a real one only when religion was associated with institutions, traditions, or symbols, but when defined as "personal self-devotion, religious feeling, fear and reverence for higher power," Jordan believed that the conflict would dissolve.[40] Nor was the conflict as it had appeared in history peculiar only to theology. The struggle of new ideas to displace tradition or precedent was common to knowledge of all kinds, and it appeared in whatever fields new discoveries ran counter to familiar opinions long held by organized bodies of men.

So Jordan now proposed to reconcile science and religion in a new fashion. Instead of insisting that scientific presuppositions provided an adequate foundation for religion, he undertook to approach the problem from the other end, giving chief attention to religion in an effort to denote its essential and creative elements. Jordan explained that both science and re-

---

[40] Jordan, "The Warfare of Science," *The Philosopher*, January–February 1924, p. 4.

ligion were partners in a common enterprise. Their purpose was, he thought, to establish a satisfactory relationship between man and the hidden or unseen aspects of the universe. "To stand in awe before the unseen is the beginning of religion, to attempt to find out how.it behaves is the beginning of science."[41] This view raised religion to a level of respectability and justified inquiry into its fundamental doctrines. In seeking such fundamentals, Jordan did not follow the lead of other scientists and turn to nature. He went directly to the teachings of Jesus where he found the central Christian affirmations to be "faith, hope, courage, and above all Love."[42] And he went even further, for he held that these teachings were expressed in explicit theological doctrines, namely, the fatherhood of God and the brotherhood of man. Meanwhile, Jordan continued to emphasize the necessity for projecting religion into life. Although " 'religion pure and undefiled' " was natural to man, he held, and " 'springs eternal in the human breast,' " it must be related to action to become real and meaningful. Another element of religion, this one, indeed, supported by the findings of science, was the assumption that an Intelligence pervaded the universe and gave it order. Since everything that exists has a cause behind it, and all change is orderly, it is necessary to posit an intelligent source of the universe to make it meaningful.[43] Jordan could insist, therefore, that faith was an essential element of religion, if the object of faith were not an accumulation of superstition and tradition.

Let us say, rather [he proposed], faith that there is in the universe some force or spirit which transcends humanity, but of which the life of man is part, not the whole, something which is intensely real and which it is well for men to recognize, for to follow its ways brings effort and action, peace and helpfulness, the sole basis of happiness.[44]

Jordan was thus much closer to the Christian tradition than were most men of science, for his theology affirmed a God which transcended man, whereas theirs recognized a deity that was immanent in nature.

The reconciliation of religion and science through a more adequate understanding of religion seemed even more likely to Jordan when he reviewed the causes of conflict and concluded that religion was not chiefly responsible for it. What had passed for a conflict of science and religion was really, Jordan thought, an antagonism of reason and reverence, caused largely by ignorance and by the association of religion in the popular mind with

[41] Jordan, "Reason, Reverence and Love," *Scientific Monthly*, December 1925, p. 590.
[42] Jordan, "Evolution and Theology," *Sunset Magazine*, March 1924, p. 15.
[43] "Reason, Reverence and Love," *Scientific Monthly*, December 1925, p. 587.
[44] *Ibid.*, p. 590.

tradition or with scientific notions now long superseded. But reason and reverence, Jordan asserted, were both legitimate human activities. And although reverence might sometimes be attached to unworthy objects, Jordan saw clearly that reason, too, was capable of misuse. In his later writing he distinguished clearly between the processes of reason and the methods of science, which he held derived rather from experimentation and induction than from the logical workings of the mind. The man of reverence was less likely to precipitate the struggle between science and religion, Jordan thought, than the philosopher or scholar who applied the laws of science to problems or materials beyond their proper competence, or than the "fundamentalist" in fields other than religion who claimed for his particular principles an absolutism or a universality that they did not possess. Fundamentalism, it was clear, was not the exclusive property of theology. Wherever it appeared it produced a conflict with science, for it was characteristic of science to present its findings modestly and to restrict them carefully to the narrow field where they properly applied.[45]

It is too much to claim that Jordan's reconciliation of science and religion by a re-examination of religious essentials, rather than by inference from scientific presuppositions, was a significant change in his point of view. Yet it illustrates from another direction his movement toward anti-intellectualism which was apparent in his earlier vitalist doctrines. This movement continued. Jordan could now say "we can know nothing until we find it out, *not think it out* [italics mine], but prove through observation or experiment its actual objective reality."[46] One could count little on powers of reason to solve the riddles of the universe. Although the methods of science, as he understood them, seemed to Jordan to promise most for the understanding of man and of his world, even these were not likely to yield the "master key" of the universe. The sciences led ultimately either to the infinitely large or to the finitely small. Jordan suspected also that the clue to the nature of the Creator would "also lie within the gates of infinity."[47] Because he believed that such knowledge was not possible, it followed that religion must make no claim to truth, and that the improvement of humankind was, therefore, the proper province for religious activity.

From the standpoint of science [Jordan stated], the question as to whether any religion is true has no meaning. Religion itself is not concerned with statements

---

[45] "Evolution and Theology," *Sunset Magazine*, March 1924, p. 15.

[46] "Reason, Reverence and Love," *Scientific Monthly*, December 1925, p. 587.

[47] "The Search for the Master Key of the Universe," *Scientific Monthly*, January 1926, p. 36.

of fact, either of science or of history. The actual problem is whether impulses, actions, or opinions, called religion, work out for human betterment.[48]

Thus Jordan's view of religion as a program for social amelioration instead of a search for truth, as a faith in a transcendant universal spirit instead of a benevolent universe, was in keeping with his increasing distrust of the intellectual processes as the foremost instrument for winning knowledge.

Jordan's last published work, *The Higher Foolishness,* was a revision of earlier writings with some added new material organized rather loosely around the theme that men prefer error to enlightenment and fall easy prey to the mountebanks who capitalize on their tacit consent to the aphorism "ignorance is bliss." The book expanded some of the discussion in *Science and Sciosophy* and introduced a new chapter on the relationship of "sciosophy" and "ecclesiasticism." Jordan was seventy-six years old when the book was published and was by that time scarcely concerned or, for that matter, able to give the subject of the relationship of science and religion more systematic treatment. But in addition to repeating much of the old argument he gave new emphasis to two elements with which he concluded the discussion. Again he made it clear that the antagonist of science was not religion, but pseudo-religion, which he now labeled ecclesiasticism.

So far, however [Jordan wrote], we have touched only indirectly upon the relation of Sciosophy, the shadow of wisdom, to Ecclesiasticism, the shadow of religion, a term which I may again define as the great body of organized, working, religious thought in its varying manifestations throughout the world.[49]

Ecclesiasticism, Jordan held, frequently assumed the character of religion itself, and it did so when it emphasized its own organization and structure or its peculiar system of doctrine or belief. Ecclesiasticism replaced religion when it organized in the name of religion to resist the progress of knowledge and to punish men who think for themselves. Thus Jordan selected for his final indictment the two elements of organization and theology. The two were very closely associated. The consensus of the group institutionalized in the religious organization gave a sanction to the authoritative doctrine. It may be that a part of Jordan's distrust for reason proceeded from his dislike of the systematic rational structures which were erected to defend the dogma of the organization. For scholasticism was the product of the school, and its representatives used reason upon dogmas held a priori and authorized by the organization for the purpose of arriving at special doctrines.

---

[48] "Reason, Reverence and Love," *Scientific Monthly,* December 1925, p. 589.
[49] *The Higher Foolishness* (Indianapolis, 1927), pp. 194–95.

Scholasticism and wisdom [Jordan held] are not identical; sometimes they are not even on speaking terms. Scholasticism looks backward to the past; wisdom looks forward to the future.[50]

Jordan believed that the essence of religion could not be reached by the methods of reason. Nor, indeed, could the truths of science. It would appear, in the end, that Jordan's distrust of the extreme claims made for reason by philosophers and scientists alike moved him to look with greater sympathy upon the somewhat irrational insights of religion.

After Jordan's retirement from the chancellorship of Stanford University, he was able to devote more time to writing for publication and to correspondence, and among his papers an accumulation of letters and unpublished fragments testify to his continued interest in the problem of the relationship of science and religion. Most of his correspondence on this subject was addressed to a few obscure men with whom he carried on a running discussion of the place of science in contemporary life. Little new in the way of insight into the problem appeared in the writing of this period. Jordan's statements repeated formulas with which he had long been familiar and frequently came as echoes of the distant past. But they did indicate the aspects of the problem to which he would give emphasis in his declining years and which had a continuing interest for him.

In one respect, however, Jordan's consideration of science and religion showed a line of development which carried a step further his modifications of the philosophy of pragmatism. Jordan had earlier proposed to widen the perspective of pragmatism in the direction of vitalism, thus making the prime test of relevance the relationship to life entire rather than to some particular problem within it. But at last he seems to have seen more clearly that so comprehensive a point of view was too broad to explain the peculiar place of man in the natural universe, and his last writings suggested a humanism which gave greater emphasis to the uniqueness of human personality. The crucial issue which seems to have been decisive for Jordan in the formulation of his humanistic doctrine was the place of the self in a broader vitalism. Jordan seems to have been aware, in the end, of the contradiction between his scientifically validated vitalism, which lost the self at a higher and more complex level of collectivity, and his common-sense humanism, which found religious sanction in the inviolability of man. This contradiction he did not adequately resolve, but so far as he had to choose between its alternatives, he found greater meaning in the religious insight than in the quantitative exactitude of science.

[50] *Ibid.*, p. 209.

Religion originated, Jordan held, in a spirit of awe, wonder, and reverence before the mysteries of the universe. From this attitude there issued two fundamental demands: one, for some kind of action; the other, for some kind of knowledge. From its concern with action, religion became the source of character.

It is now believed that the realities of Religion are shown in human conduct [Jordan wrote]. Men who have faith in religion as the mainspring of character, as a reverent dependence on the ways of the power that creates and recreates the Universe, can never lose their faith.[51]

Such a faith supported moral action and in turn grew stronger as human character itself reached a higher level of morality. Man's feeling of awe before the universe, however, demanded something more than moral activity and the development of character. It demanded an intellectual explanation of the mystery which inspired it. Such a demand, Jordan believed, could not be satisfied by any expression of authority. Ultimately the intellect and the senses must show the inadequacy of any authoritative explanation regarding the nature of the creation. Men must have faith, therefore, not only that duty brings happiness, which is morality, but that the universe is rationally intelligible, which makes the pursuit of knowledge by science a meaningful occupation.[52]

Religion required, according to Jordan, the recognition of and the reverence for an intelligence which pervaded the universe. But such a simple recognition of intelligibility in the universe is capable of varied manifestations and much corruption. For this reason, Jordan felt, "religion" produces many "religions." The historic religions seized upon some incidental characteristic prominent for a time in the religious behavior of their group and made it an essential element around which their representatives formed an organization. Thus tradition, symbolism, poetry, creed, ceremonials, a source of authority, or a particular form of organization had at one time or another provided the nuclei for various "religions." These elements quickly acquired authority and soon turned into superstition, which Jordan defined as "believing what you know is not true."

Religio naturally runs into superstitions, from which only science (that is, tested human experience) can save it. But superstitions die, the spirit of awe and wonder never.[53]

[51] David Starr Jordan to Members of the Congregational Church Extension Committee, Los Angeles, December 24, 1923, Jordan Correspondence, Vol. LXXXIV.
[52] Jordan to G. Bacon Price, March 14, 1924, *ibid.*, Vol. LXXXIV.
[53] Jordan to J. Arthur Eddy, June 14, 1924, *ibid.*, Vol. LXXXIV.

Hence, it should be the function of science to distill the essential *religio* from the mass of superstition embodied in the various historic religions.

Jordan's humanism began with the fundamental assumption that man is a proper source of knowledge of God because the religious function—that is to say, man's innate capacity for awe and reverence—is an essential function of man's natural personality. Thus, said Jordan, "every robust life is a life of faith; not in details of what some one has said, but faith in God and his prophets."[54] Indeed, every good man is a prophet of God. From the evidence of " 'lives made beautiful and sweet by self-devotion and by self-restraint,' " Jordan argued, one may infer an attribute of God. But suppose someone answered that such attributes are merely characteristics of humanity, not qualities of God. Jordan replied, "Who knows that this is not, in fact, the same thing?"[55]

But, for Jordan, humanism was not only the central characteristic of religion in general; it was also the essential element of Christianity. "Jesus taught us to worship God through faith in man," Jordan wrote.[56] He emphasized the sanctity of human personality, exalting human values, and teaching that man is free to control his character, his hopes, and his acts. Therefore, Jordan concluded, "genuine Christianity cannot rest on any form of oppression or suppression,"[57] but insists upon human freedom and issues finally in that ultimate freedom, the integrity of the human mind.[58] Jordan's movement from vitalism to humanism was accompanied by the reassertion of an element of rational intelligibility which had earlier been obscured by his discovery that a vitalist philosophy provided a broader context than pragmatism for the findings of experimental science.

With rational intelligibility as the fundamental presupposition alike for Jordan's view of the universe and of man, it followed easily that a congenial view of God must see Him also as an intelligible Being. For if the objective universe is indeed intelligible but is not intelligible to man, it is necessary to provide a comprehending Mind within whose insights the universe can achieve rationality and order. Jordan's analysis begins with the fact of man's confronting the universe, and seeking unity and order within it:

Our experience with the objective universe and its effects on our subjective consciousness, seems to imply the existence of a still larger consciousness, in which

---

[54] Jordan to M. J. Bradshaw, March 28, 1923, *ibid.*, Vol. LXXXIV.

[55] Jordan, "What is God?" (unpublished typescript), pp. [1], 3, *ibid.*, Vol. LXXI.

[56] Jordan, "A Call to Service" (unpublished typescript), p. [2], *ibid.*, Vol. LXXI.

[57] Jordan, "Authority and Sympathy" (subtitle; unpublished typescript), p. 6, *ibid.*, Vol. LXXI.

[58] Jordan to G. Bacon Price, January 3, 1923, *ibid.*, Vol. LXXXIV.

objective and subjective should be united. The objective universe should be within
the grasp of some intelligence. The final answer to the world problem cannot be
disconnected, disjointed matter and force in unrelated fragments. The universe is
too gigantic, too complex, too exact in its relation of cause and effect, too conscien-
tious in its rewards and punishment, to exist in our consciousness alone. There
seems to be outside ourselves, as well as within, a compelling "force that makes for
righteousness." Outside ourselves is "the ceaseless flow of energy and the rational
intelligence that pervades it." No part of this flow of force can we fully comprehend, but we can realize its persistence and the consistency of its methods. We find
no chance movement in the universe, "no variableness, no shadow of turning."
That there should exist a "law of Heaven and Earth whose way is solid, substantial, vast, and unchanging," seems to imply an intelligence adequate to have made
it so, and to comprehend it as a whole, not merely as shown in casual and inexorable
fragments. This intelligence should deal with terms of absolute truth, freed from
all figures of speech drawn from human experience, and of all anthropomorphism
imposed by the limitations of human action. Only a "God of the things as they are"
can "know things as they really are," and in our relations to these things, we become conscious of the condition of being, gracious and inexorable, the "Goodness
and Severity of God."[59]

Thus the quest for intelligibility and morality in an immense and complicated
universe had led Jordan at last to the concept of a transcendent and comprehending God, a God of life as it was actually lived, a "God of the things as
they are."

The same quest, together with his impatience with such externals of
religion as creed, tradition, or ceremonial, led Jordan also to favor a policy
of broad toleration toward religious differences rather than a movement to
compromise them and unite Christian denominations. He viewed creeds as
statements of fact which were the concern of science rather than of religion.[60]
Even the differences between Jew and Christian, so far as Jordan could see,
were negligible. Indeed, contemporary Christianity involved much that he
would not care to ask Jews to adopt. Instead, he suggested,

I should advise not trying to convert a Jewish friend to Christianity, but would lay
stress on possible agreements, whereof there are plenty. I find certain Jews . . .
just as good Christians as I could ask for.[61]

Religious antagonisms were simply not compatible with a rationally intelligible universe, and Jordan believed that the God of the humanists, faithful

---

[59] Jordan, "Religion and Science" (unpublished typescript), pp. 44–46, Jordan Correspondence, Vol. LXXI.

[60] Jordan to Ralph W. Brown, June 18, 1925, ibid., Vol. LXXXIV.

[61] Jordan to George Gilmour, June 1, 1929, ibid., Vol. LXXXV. This is perhaps Jordan's
last statement on a religious subject.

to the principles of fatherhood and brotherhood, would not permit them to shatter the unity of the catholic commonwealth.

Whereas on the one hand the legitimate product of humanistic religion was moral conduct, on the other hand it was trustworthy knowledge. An attitude of awe and reverence toward the universe, Jordan held, led as surely toward one as toward the other. The proper province of religion was character, together with the formulation of basic propositions regarding the nature of man and the characteristics of deity. But taking as its fundamental presupposition the intelligibility of the universe, the religious attitude, according to Jordan, led to the methods and processes by means of which knowledge was verified and systematized—that is, to science. "Science," Jordan held, "is human experience tested and set in order."[62] Jordan believed that there was a great gulf between science and philosophy, which he described as

the penumbra of guesses, plausible or not, derived from what we actually know, from what we think we would like to know, or what somebody knowing less than we do has guessed in the past.[63]

Notions that might be regarded as related to philosophy Jordan considered as related, instead, to science, and he looked to science rather than to philosophy for the analysis and testing of articles of belief or bodies of knowledge. Similarly, science must be distinguished from religion. Science, Jordan held, is objective and impersonal and deals with outer reality, whereas religion, being subjective, is concerned with inner feelings.[64] It was clear to Jordan that science posited as a fundamental presupposition the existence of an objective reality external to mind, and that the findings of science were legitimate only when they emerged from the investigation of real problems. "Our knowledge of all truth is conditioned on the one most marvelous of all," he wrote, "that we reach some actual reality and that we know that we do this."[65] Many of the errors attributed to science were rather the consequence of setting up unreal or meaningless problems. Even the agnosticism associated with science, Jordan thought, would disappear the moment it became involved in a real problem. "Gravitation may be agnostic until something drops," Jordan observed. "Love, also, until reality gets at the other end of it."[66]

When Jordan translated his humanism into a theory of knowledge he was

[62] Jordan to G. Bacon Price, March 14, 1924, *ibid.*, Vol. LXXXIV.
[63] Jordan to Scudder Klyce, October 8, 1923, *ibid.*, Vol. LXXXV.
[64] Jordan to J. Helder, March 23, 1927, *ibid.*, Vol. LXXXIV.
[65] Jordan, "Prefatory Note" [to a manuscript by Danziger] (unpublished typescript), p. 6, *ibid.*, Vol. LXXI.
[66] Jordan to Scudder Klyce, April 3, 1924, *ibid.*, Vol. LXXXIII.

compelled to hold that all truth was relative, that the only truth available to man was human truth. "Humanly speaking," he wrote, "and there is no other way for us to try to speak, there is no absolute truth."[67] No proposition could be true, Jordan thought, from all standpoints at once, and when anyone asserted that something was true, he meant only that if the truth were acted upon, it would be followed by anticipated results. This was the familiar epistemology of pragmatism. Scientific truth was necessarily approximate truth because its premises were imperfect and changing, whereas the so-called absolute truth of mathematics was not an addition to knowledge at all but merely an exploration of the consequences of knowledge already gained by observation and experiment.[68] But Jordan was not content to rest on the assertion that all truth was tentative. Although he recognized that man could not obtain the whole truth about anything, he asserted that such truth as man had was indeed absolute and ultimate:

We can never know the complete truth . . . but what we do know may be just as real, just as true, as though we knew it all. It is the truth as far as it goes, and the truth, man-truth, in our possession, is just as true as tho it were God's truth, which, indeed, it is as well.[69]

Thus for the truths of science, stated in terms of previous human experience, Jordan was willing to claim "actual verity so far as they go."[70] Because Jordan presupposed an objective reality and believed that through the methods of science man could actually touch it and come away with absolute truth, he departed considerably from the more limited theory of knowledge of pragmatism.

In another respect also Jordan's views on the nature of truth differed from those of other pragmatists. For Jordan held not only that so much of truth as man actually had was absolute and ultimate, but also that this truth was verified not by its "workableness" or its "intelligibility" but by its "livableness." The tests of workableness, intelligibility, and livableness are, indeed, all humanistic criteria of truth, for they apply to man's work, man's intelligence, and man's life. Jordan would agree that truth must work, and that truth must be intelligible. As he put it, "When Knowledge is put into terms of human experience it becomes intelligible—that is, it becomes Truth, and to use it in life constitutes wisdom."[71] But both work and intelligence were understood

[67] "Religion and Science" (unpublished typescript), p. 11, Jordan Correspondence, Vol. LXXI.
[68] Jordan to R. A. Millikan, July 27, 1923, ibid., Vol. LXXXIII.
[69] "Religion and Science" (unpublished typescript), p. 19, ibid., Vol. LXXI.
[70] Ibid., p. 5.
[71] Jordan to Lynde Denig, January 22, 1924, ibid., Vol. LXXXIV.

by Jordan to serve the enrichment of life, so that his humanism was interpreted in vitalist rather than in instrumentalist or rationalist terms. "Whatever cannot be lived, is not yet true," he insisted.[72] Workableness, although not to be repudiated as a test of truth, was nevertheless inadequate from the wider perspective of Jordan's humanism. The fact that an idea happens to work, Jordan argued, was no guaranty of its truth. Ideas are often made to work by people who are determined to make them do so; for men are themselves involved in the application of their ideas, and their devotion and energy are oftentimes more responsible for the outcome than the validity of the proposition they may happen to employ as an instrument. Nor is any proposition as a whole ever completely validated by the consequences of applying it. Science must itself determine, Jordan insisted, exactly what aspects of a truth are really responsible for its successful working, and these may be quite other than what its proponents deem essential.[73] And finally, within the narrow requirements of workableness there is no assurance, Jordan maintained, that a proposition, so validated, would lead to the enhancement of life. And so again Jordan allows a note of absolutism to temper the pragmatic doctrine that all truth is relative. Workableness is a test satisfactory only in the short run. A proposition might be workable and yet so fraught with error that although it

might not involve actual race extinction, at least not within an appreciable time . . . it would involve destruction in proportion to the importance of the error. For the rest we might expect that life would be on a lower plane than would be possible with more exact knowledge and the courage and intellect to make use of it.[74]

To be adequate for the preservation of the race and for life on a higher plane our knowledge must be "true so far as it goes, and so far as it concerns us," not just true enough to satisfy the requirements of a particular situation. Despite his emphasis upon the tentativity of scientific truth, Jordan was well aware that for the achievement of ultimate ends men must formulate and commit themselves to absolute truths.

If in the final analysis Jordan found scientific truth inadequate for ultimate problems, he likewise found the scientific description of man's nature inapplicable to the real situations in which man was involved in life and history. Man could, indeed, be reduced to the terms of physics or of biology, but when that was done, Jordan believed, nothing had been accomplished save

[72] "Religion and Science" (unpublished typescript), p. 48, ibid., Vol. LXXI.
[73] Ibid., pp. 22–23.
[74] Jordan, untitled typescript, pp. 17–18, ibid., Vol. LXXI.

a change in nomenclature. And the enterprise was not without considerable danger, for in analyzing the interdependence of cells and organs, the concept of the self was likely to be lost. The vitalist view of man was presented by Jordan with an air of plausibility:

Physically each man is an alliance of zooids, of energides, of centers of proto-plasmic action; each so-called cell, or energide, a sort of quasi-individual organism; each member of this alliance having its own processes of life, growth, death, and reproduction; each one with its own cell-soul, which in some unknown fashion presides over all these processes. In the alliance of these cells forming tissues and organs, we have the phenomena of mutual help and mutual dependence. We have these also in the phenomena of human society. In man these features of organic life are seen on a larger and more complex scale than in the lower forms, but an analysis of these phenomena in either case leaves little meaning to the word "self." "I think, therefore I am" gives place to "we think, therefore we are." But that again is not true; for we think only as co-operating groups of centers of energy, not as individual units of life. The self or ego is an attribute of one changing alliance as set off against another. What is the vital force which holds this alliance together? What is vitalism as distinct from mechanism? Is either anything more than a name for the chemical attributes of complex changing organic molecules?[75]

But Jordan did not find the vitalist view of man particularly meaningful, nor did he believe that he was obliged to provide a theory of man's nature. "It does not occur to me that it is necessary to answer such questions as 'What is Man?'" he wrote to one correspondent; " . . . you might take it for granted."[76] Yet his own view of man was clearly stated in much that he wrote. Although he might hesitate to say that man was God's crowning work, he found him superior to other created things by virtue of his versatility: "Personally I should say that even a small man was a greater creation than a very big tree; if he did not last so long, he could do more things."[77] And what was most important, Jordan's scientific proclivity for analysis did not tempt him to overlook man's integrity in the multiplicity of his parts. He regarded men as individuals, that is, as unities which could not be divided into parts. He insisted that in studies of individual men one must even abandon the methods of analysis and the common facts of "psychology, physiology, evolution, and existence," in order that "the unit we are looking after" and "the purposes for which we are writing" may not be obscured.[78] To such lengths did Jordan

[75] Jordan, untitled typescript, Jordan Correspondence, Vol. LXXI, 36–37.

[76] Jordan to J. E. Gibson, August 1, 1923, ibid., Vol. LXXXIV.

[77] Ibid.

[78] Jordan to Scudder Klyce, October 9, 1923, ibid., Vol. LXXXIII.

go in order that the habitual approaches of the scientist might not do injustice to the integrity of man's nature.

Jordan's view of the relationship of science and religion was set forth in his early writings and changed little in the course of his later correspondence. With religion defined as the attitude of awe and reverence toward the mysteries of the universe and with science as human experience tested and systematized, with ultimate validity for the enhancement of life, there would seem on the surface little likelihood of conflict or need of reconciliation between them. Jordan believed throughout his life that nothing inherent in either science or religion inevitably involved them in conflict. But that conflict had existed was a fact of history. For the historic conflict of science and religion, Jordan held, the usual explanation was the propensity of interested individuals and organizations to give to partial truths or, indeed, even to errors a degree of absolutism not warranted by scientific methods of validation. Jordan did not insist that scientific truth was wholly relative and contingent, and he was not prepared, therefore, to attack as presumptuous the assertion that at certain points human truth was equivalent to the truth of God. But whenever men claimed for scientific truth a validity which science could not substantiate, then conflict was bound to arise.

Jordan did not believe that it was possible to formulate any statement about the universe or man's relation to it which would be equally meaningful to men at all times and in all places. Truths necessarily deteriorated with age, so that even the great utterances of Jesus had become corrupted by the errors of later interpreters.[79] Consequently, whenever a party arose to assert that a truth was absolute and to promulgate it, error was inevitably perpetuated. Heretical movements eventually appeared to challenge in dialectical fashion the validity of the authoritative formulation, and the heretics stated their rival notions as creeds which sometimes even won endorsement from the privileged authority. In the continuing conflict, it was the function of science, Jordan believed, to distinguish between elements of truth and error. "Scientific men," he held, "are the real defenders of the faith and . . . all creeds in their day were written by heretics whose successors hung on too long after the crisis was past."[80] Thus the conflict between science and religion was best described, Jordan thought, as a "struggle between living theories and dying ones" marked by "the constant effort to support moribund notions by investing them with divine authority."[81] Although Jordan was not unfriendly toward statements

---

[79] Jordan to G. Bacon Price, January 20, 1927, *ibid.*, Vol. LXXXIV.
[80] Jordan to J. B. Sunderland, March 2, 1925, *ibid.*, Vol. LXXXIV.
[81] "Religion and Science" (unpublished typescript), p. 57, *ibid.*, Vol. LXXI.

of religious doctrine, he was never able to comprehend any sanction for truth other than verification by scientific method. Therefore his objection to religious propositions was not that they claimed divine authority but that they disregarded scientific validation. The newest theory, he thought, was most likely to be the correct one; so the conflict between science and religion in its simplest form was the eternal struggle between new truth seeking validation and older truth, whose partisans refused to modify it. There was little that men could or should do to mitigate such a conflict, Jordan thought, for the progress of scientific investigation would correct error and refine truth. "I haven't much use for the views of any 'reconciler'," he wrote one correspondent.[82] Nonetheless, he looked forward to a final reconciliation, for he believed that in the processes of nature he could see indications of an eventual divine harmony.

In the world process of human evolution [Jordan wrote], as already indicated, there are three divine culminations, reason, duty and love. Arising from different sources, or from different parts of the same source, they come together at the end and through them we can reach the ultimate reconciliation of religion, emotion and science.[83]

Jordan's final judgment on the warfare of science and religion was that it was not a serious conflict and that men should not be concerned about it. Jordan took his place, in the end, as the transitional figure in a half-century of discussion of the relationship of science and religion. He saw the conflict in much the same terms as his predecessors, and he believed that his explanation would soften its antagonisms. For the time being, the optimism characteristic of American life in the decade of the 1920's obscured the sources of conflict which made the relationship of science and religion a much more serious problem for Jordan's successors.

The controversy over the teaching of evolution in the public schools, which culminated in the Scopes trial at Dayton, Tennessee, in 1925, gave Jordan an opportunity to illustrate his views on the conflict of science and religion. Jordan thought it unfortunate that the controversy, which was narrowly limited to a question of what to teach in the high schools, should have been presented to the popular mind as an essential conflict of religion and science, for thereby it raised false issues and did great disservice to both science and religion. Fundamentalism was not peculiar to religious thought, Jordan believed, but was characteristic of the attitude of any group of men who

[82] Jordan to Scudder Klyce, n.d., Jordan Correspondence, Vol. LXXXIII.
[83] Jordan, untitled typescript, p. 22, *ibid.*, Vol. LXXI.

claimed validity for their doctrines beyond the power of scientific method to substantiate them. The dogma of Biblical inerrancy was an example of the absolutism which science was obliged to destroy wherever it appeared. Therefore the controversy did not involve any essential Christian notions but only those of the fundamentalists, who were indeed correct in recognizing that science was antagonistic to them.

No doubt the Fundamentalists are right [Jordan wrote] in assuming that all forms of science and of the literary and philosophic phases of Darwinism are truly subversive of *their notions* [italics mine] of Christianity.[84]

Nor, on the other hand, did the controversy truly present the views of science. For several years before the trial at Dayton, William Jennings Bryan in many popular speeches and published articles had misrepresented, Jordan thought, what scientists really believed about the origin and development of life on the earth. Jordan described the views which Bryan attributed to science as "theories once apparently workable, but which with better knowledge have long since ceased to work." If the scientific conception of evolution was what Bryan thought it was, said Jordan, "it would be as hateful to me as it is to him."[85] Bryan was not making a real challenge to the position of science because the issues he raised were long since dead.

The trouble with Bryant [*sic*] and his kind [Jordan wrote] is not that they oppose living science, but that they are apostles of dead science, thoroughly and absolutely dead.[86]

Jordan was confident that scientific inquiry would be able to defend its views against the representatives of notions long since discarded, and therefore he did not greatly fear the popular support which Bryan was winning for fundamentalism and pseudo science.

In appraising the fundamentalist controversy, Jordan again emphasized the fact that the danger lay not so much in popularizing erroneous notions about science and religion as in claiming for them a false degree of absolutism and in supporting them by law. Guarantee the freedom of inquiry, and truth would win out, Jordan believed, even over "the gross ignorance of Mr. Bryan . . ." His opposition was directed rather "against those who would use the law to suppress the teaching of truth,"[87] and against Bryan's absolutism, his "attitude of knowing all, when he has only emotional attitudes toward what

[84] Jordan to Maynard Shipley, June 22, 1927, *ibid.*, Vol. LXXXIV.
[85] Jordan to Scudder Klyce, October 23, 1923, *ibid.*, Vol. LXXXIII.
[86] Jordan to Scudder Klyce, November 9, 1923, *ibid.*, Vol. LXXXIII.
[87] Jordan to Charles T. Sprading, June 5, 1925, *ibid.*, Vol. LXXXIV.

he never tried to understand."[88] The only weapon which one need employ in the fight against all kinds of fundamentalism, Jordan believed, was the diligent search for facts and the honest publication of them when found. "To my mind," he insisted, "the facts are more important than the conclusions. When you get facts enough, anybody can draw conclusions."[89] It was characteristic of Jordan's generation to underestimate man's perversity in drawing false conclusions even from facts scrupulously verified by the most exact methods of science and to overestimate the ability of truth to prevail over error when error, rather than truth, had the more substantial support of the human will and human resources.

Throughout his life Jordan showed a marked gift for aphoristic statement. The correspondence of his last years contained many of his favorite aphorisms which often indicated more pointedly than his arguments his basic convictions on the proper place of religion and science. Against all pretensions to absolutism, he frequently asserted the impermanence of life and history: "Nothing endures save the flow of energy and the rational order that pervades it." In such a universe only science can be trusted to provide guidance to man, for "Science is human experience tested and set in order." Of knowledge, however, "We know nothing until we find it out." The final test of truth is its liveableness: "It is true if we can trust our lives to it." This test applied also, Jordan held, to beliefs about right and wrong. Truth will ultimately prevail, but not by argument: "Old errors do not die out because they are refuted; they fade out when neglected."

The course of truth is generally impeded, Jordan thought, by theological dogmas. Therefore he often quoted Huxley's statement to the effect that "Extinguished theologians lie about the cradle of every infant science like the strangled snakes about that of the infant Hercules." For "Science is criticism, religion is emotion." By this definition religion was justified because "Every man needs a pillar to lean against and a bosom to weep into." The function of religion was to develop character: "In all ages and climes lives have been made beautiful by self-devotion and self-restraint." From this point of view "Religions die, religion never," for, following Emerson, "At the last nothing is sacred save the integrity of your own mind."

All life is an adventure which requires the fullest participation from each man and promises only the sense of satisfaction which comes from devotion freely given. "Believe and venture." Do not ask for assurances: "As for

[88] Jordan to Scudder Klyce, December 10, 1923, Jordan Correspondence, Vol. LXXXIII.
[89] Jordan to Charles T. Sprading, June 5, 1925, *ibid.*, Vol. LXXXIV.

pledges, the gods give none." Rely, therefore, on "the goodness and severity of God." In the final analysis a religion was to be judged by its fruits: "The best test of religion is the one offered by Jesus to Peter: 'Feed my lambs.' "

What was perhaps Jordan's most frequently quoted maxim distinguished between wisdom, virtue, and religion. "Wisdom," he said, "is knowing what one ought to do next; virtue is doing it; religion is the reason why." To this he added, in *The Days of a Man*, "and prayer, the core of our endeavor."[90]

[90] Jordan, *The Days of a Man* (New York, 1922), II, 773.

6

Naturalism Versus Supernaturalism
John Dewey

FOR THE HIATUS between science and religion in recent American thought no one bears more responsibility than John Dewey. Dewey's philosophical exertions have been devoted largely to examining the relationship between facts and values. It is therefore paradoxical in the extreme that although he has attempted to reduce facts and values to a common naturalistic basis, an effort which won wide support in its initial stages, he has suceeded only in widening the breach and in giving more pronounced emphasis to the irreducible and unique element in religious experience. Dewey's analysis of the relationship of science and religion is presented in the most persuasive terms and embedded in the most rigorous dialectic of any American philosopher. He claims for his naturalistic ethics all the virtues of Christian morals and consistently denies to religious absolutes any proper place in moral philosophy. Dewey is par excellence the philosopher of the world of contingencies. In so far as religion has to do with man's relationship to absolutes and ultimates, Dewey cannot be said to have any religious philosophy at all.

Almost no one illustrates better than John Dewey the extent to which philosophical thought may reflect the character of the social and historical milieu in which it happens to be formulated. Dewey's early manhood embraced the two decades of agrarian revolt at the end of the nineteenth century which provided the dynamic for the Populists and the platform for the Progressives. Because better than anyone of his generation he stated the ideals of a life at once democratic and preoccupied with the contingent necessities of a material culture, he became the philosophical spokesman and prophet for the young American liberals whose world was shattered at Sarajevo in June 1914.[1] These years saw the formulation of those doctrines in the philosophy of education and ethics which appeared in 1916 as *Democracy and Education* and in 1922 as *Human Nature and Conduct*. To the presuppositions of American social democracy Dewey added those of the scientific revolution

---

[1] See Alfred Kazin, *On Native Grounds: An Interpretation of Modern American Prose Literature* (New York, 1942), p. 145.

of the age of Darwin and Huxley. Born in the year of publication of *The Origin of Species*, Dewey carried through life a preoccupation with the methods of science and brought science and democracy into a juxtaposition from which he somehow concluded their inherent and necessary correlation. The philosopher of democracy and science taught that education in a democratic society implied that the classroom must become a miniature democracy, and society at large a scientific laboratory for experiments in democracy. These principles Dewey gradually extended, applying them in hundreds of published writings to all aspects of thought. The systematization and interpretation of his philosophical doctrine in its general outlines he achieved in three series of public lectures between 1925 and 1934. In the lectures on the Paul Carus Foundation in 1925, *Experience and Nature*, he developed his view of the empirical basis of metaphysics; in the Gifford Lectures at Edinburgh in 1929, *The Quest for Certainty*, he described the relationship between a theory of knowledge and the practical consequences of action; and in his lectures at Yale in 1933 on the Terry Foundation, *A Common Faith*, he applied his doctrines to an analysis of the origin and practical effects of "religious" ideals.

In spite of Dewey's association of his instrumentalism (the doctrine that ideas are instruments for the achievement of planned results and are to be judged true or false only in relationship to those results) with the broad stream of pragmatic thought, which originated with Charles Peirce and was popularized by William James, his kinship in dealing with the problem of science and religion would seem to lie rather with the older tradition of Draper and White. For whereas James's pluralism permitted him to appreciate the validity of ideals apart from any assumption of their naturalistic origin, Dewey's monism obliged him to wage destructive war on doctrines, institutions, and ritual forms which could not be associated with nature either as a source or as an end in accommodating the individual to the total universe.

The conflict between science and religion as Dewey saw it had, nonetheless, advanced beyond the lines of battle laid down by Draper and White. The problem no longer involved an antagonism between the findings of science and the older beliefs of religion about the mechanics of heavenly bodies, the structure of the earth, or the development and physiology of the human species. Instead, the fundamental conflict is seen as an antagonism between facts and values. The development of the natural sciences is said to have revealed an incompatibility between the conclusions of science and the realm of higher values, of ideal and spiritual qualities. Dewey attacks the view that science has stripped the world of its beauty and its morality by presenting nature "as a scene of indifferent physical particles acting according to mathematical and mechanical laws."[2] He also holds persons who raise the question of the relationship of science and religion to be suspect for trying either to use the knowledge of science to substantiate religious beliefs or to derogate that knowledge to make room for the undisputed sway of religious dogma. A further danger, one to which Dewey himself is open but which he does not discuss, is that of imposing the presuppositions of science to the point of destroying the valid insights of religion.

What mistakenly appeared, then, as a conflict between facts and values impelled modern philosophy to seek a solution. The device which modern philosophy has employed, Dewey thinks, is to reverse the historic relationship between the theory of knowledge and the theory of nature. The ancient Greeks, for example, had explained the nature of knowledge by what they believed about the nature of the universe. But modern philosophy has done just the opposite. Beginning with theories regarding the nature of knowledge, modern philosophers have held their theories of the universe as secondary or derived. This, according to Dewey, instead of healing the crisis has served only to accentuate it, for it has resulted in separating the realm of values from that of facts by so great a distance that it is no longer possible for values to achieve any active participation in the world of facts and practical action.

In consequence of this inversion of the proper relationship between metaphysics and epistemology, Western society, Dewey believes, has been plunged into a "genuine cultural crisis . . . a social crisis, historical and temporal in character."[3] This crisis, which one of Dewey's interpreters calls "the great philosophic separation,"[4] runs like a chasm through modern culture. Instead of relating its values to the contingencies of developing life, modern philosophy has made them depend for their power upon the existence of some antecedent reality. Thus "the reality and power of whatever is excellent and worthy of supreme devotion," Dewey states, "depend[s] upon proof of its antecedent existence . . ."[5] The result is that modern philosophy is led away from the real problem with which it should be concerned—the problem of the cultural crisis and its cure—to the remote and academic problem of how the objects of science can be characterized as mathematical and mechanistic at the same time that the ultimate reality is properly described as ideal and spiritual. But

[2] John Dewey, *The Quest for Certainty: A Study of the Relation of Knowledge and Action*, pp. 40–41.

[3] *Ibid.*, p. 47.

[4] Joseph Ratner (ed.), *Intelligence in the Modern World: John Dewey's Philosophy* (New York, 1939), p. xi.

[5] *The Quest for Certainty*, p. 304.

the real crisis—the crisis in contemporary culture—is, Dewey insists, a crisis in the location of authority:

Scientific inquiry seems to tell one thing, and traditional beliefs about ends and ideals that have authority over conduct tell us something quite different. The problem of reconciliation arises and persists for one reason only. As long as the notions persist that knowledge is a disclosure of reality, of reality prior to and independent of knowing, and that knowing is independent of a purpose to control the quality of experienced objects, the failure of natural science to disclose significant values in its objects will come as a shock. Those seriously concerned with the validity and authority of value will have a problem on their hands. As long as the notion persists that values are authentic and valid only on condition that they are properties of Being independent of human action, as long as it is supposed that their right to regulate action is dependent upon their being independent of action, so long there will be needed schemes to prove that values are, in spite of the findings of science, genuine and known qualifications of reality in itself. For men will not easily surrender all regulative guidance in action. If they are forbidden to find standards in the course of experience they will seek them somewhere else, if not in revelation, then in the deliverance of a reason that is above experience.[6]

But if an abstract, metaphysical idealism tends to make values incapable of participating in a world of practical consequences where they have no ground or relevance, Dewey was equally clear that social Darwinism worked to the same end. The doctrine of universal evolution, that the perfect adjustment of man to the environment would eliminate all evil, is an attempt to bring value within the fold of nature in the same fashion that the idealist solutions attempt to bring nature within the fold of value. Both cases exhibit the familiar primacy of knowledge over nature, for in both a presupposition of necessary knowledge is employed to prove that value has a real and certain existence.

The ascription of value to antecedently hypothesized reality—the fundamental error, for Dewey, of modern philosophy—did not at first seem to involve philosophy in a contradiction severe enough to produce a conflict between religious absolutes and the contingencies of science. This doctrine assumed that investigation of the ultimate reality would reveal value characteristics as a necessary part of its structure and constitution. For a time, natural science gave no offence to this conception. But the investigations of the biologists in the nineteenth century and the physicists in the twentieth, giving attention to the basic constituents of life and of matter, failed to disclose in the objects of knowledge the possession of any such properties. This, Dewey believed, had precipitated the crisis between science and religion, which could

6 *Ibid.*, pp. 43–44.

be relieved only by wresting values from the realm of antecedent being, where science would not substantiate them, and relocating them in the realm of life, where their proof would lie in their consequences.

Although modern science has been responsible for subjecting the philosophical system to pressures which revealed the fatal fissure between its theories of nature and of knowledge, the disjunction, Dewey believed, ran far back into the past and could be explained only in the light of history. The source of the separation of philosophy from the practical arts lay in the aristocratic tradition, which in Greek society dignified philosophical speculation while denigrating as of a servile status the ordinary activities of practical life. Thus Aristotle ranked the social arts lower than pure intellectual inquiry, lower than knowledge not to be put to any use, not even a social and moral one. Dewey believes that this point of view might have remained nothing more than the special pleading of a small class of professional philosophers had it not been for the collapse of classical culture and the emergence of the Church as the dominant power in Europe. The Church appropriated to itself this conception of philosophic monopoly; it elevated theology to the status of "science" in the sense of a unique, comprehensive, and immutable body of doctrine over which it exercised exclusive control and guardianship; and by virtue of its influence over the hearts and conduct of the Christian community, it clothed these doctrines with an authority that the mere philosopher could never claim. This was the situation when the rise of experimental science in the sixteenth century sought to restore the knowledge of nature as fundamental to the theory of knowledge. But by this time the old tradition in philosophy, that of an antecedent reality which justified value, had become embedded in Christian theology, so that the conflict between the new experimental science and the idealist tradition in philosophy with respect to the claim to know reality was converted into a rivalry between the spiritual values affirmed by the Church and the conclusions of natural knowledge. In this conflict every advance of science seemed an encroachment upon the domain which philosophy claimed as its own and theology guarded as sacrosanct. Thus religous tradition affirmed the more positively that ultimate values were a matter of spiritual revelation and were not amenable to the methods by which the practical arts embodied their purposes in real life.[7] It was therefore scarcely to be presumed, Dewey thought, that science could have been able to regain for values a participation in life when

for over two thousand years the weight of the most influential and authoritatively

---

[7] *The Quest for Certainty,* pp. 28–29.

orthodox tradition of thought has been thrown into the opposite scale. It has been devoted to the problem of a purely cognitive certification (perhaps by revelation, perhaps by intuition, perhaps by reason) of the antecedent immutable reality of truth, beauty and goodness. As against such a doctrine, the conclusions of natural science constitute the materials of a serious problem.[8]

This tradition represented a combination of forces by the ecclesiastical authority and by the venerated classical tradition, and it remained for modern science in a revolution similar in the importance of its consequences to that of Copernicus to point the way to its dissolution.

The consequences of the crisis, Dewey felt, were too great to be lightly dismissed. In the first place, it was clearly exhibited in the failure to take those religious and moral standards which claimed antecedent reality as their warrant and apply them to concrete problems of practical life. The inapplicability of such abstract belief and judgments testified to the isolation of philosophy from life. Again, the situation approached "intellectual confusion, practically chaos" when it became apparent that old beliefs and principles capable of regulating criticism and formulating ends or ideals had dissolved, leaving nothing to take their place. Such a situation could be described only as "the absence of intellectual authority" for framing judgments and reaching conclusions about things of most vital importance.[9] Third, the outcome for philosophy has been disastrous, since, like religion, it too has come into conflict with the natural sciences over its claim to know a more ultimate reality than theirs. The separation of facts and values has thus tempted philosophy to a pretension to knowledge which has led to the assertion that the sciences deal not with a world of reality but with appearances.[10] And finally, the separation limits the sphere of science to industry and commerce and merely "secular" affairs. Dewey believed that the gain to civilization would be inestimable if the methods and insights of science could be devoted to the systematic analysis of value problems and to the formulation of programs for the incorporation of value in life. He believed that the only hope for narrowing the breach between science and religion lay in the acceptance by religion of the methods of science, for the history of the conflict seemed to Dewey to show that, unless they were accepted, the territory occupied by mundane and secular affairs, in which the guidance of science is acknowledged, would encroach more and more upon the domain claimed by religion.[11]

[8] *Ibid.*, p. 43.
[9] *Ibid.*, pp. 70–71.
[10] *Ibid.*, pp. 309–10.
[11] *Ibid.*, p. 305.

In the final analysis, then, the conflict between fact and value, between science and religion, between the reality of participation and the reality of projection—this conflict resolved into a simple conflict of methods; and the basic question was: By what method is "any and every item of intellectual belief . . . to be arrived at and justified?"[12] Dewey is fighting the old battle when he asserts that the ultimate conflict is the conflict between the method of science and allegiance to the authority of a belief, however small, which is fixed so firmly in advance that it can never be modified. For the acceptance of the methods of science implies that they will be put to actual use in testing truths and in realizing values. Modern philosophy, however, had failed to do this, and there lay the trouble. Instead of associating their ideas about values with practical activity, men had related them to the cognition of antecedent Being.[13] In other words, the modern mind had accepted the conclusions of scientific inquiry but not its method. This would have led to "remaking the conceptions of mind, knowledge and the character of the object of knowledge" by the methods of science. It would have led to the rejection of the dualistic metaphysics which separated the objects that are known by science from the values that furnish the norm and end of human destiny.[14] The idea of the two-realm scheme had perished for science, but it had persisted for moral and religious purposes. It was Dewey's contention, therefore, that the only remedy for the modern crisis lay in the extension of the philosophy of the new science into all the realms of human experience, and particularly into those which, under the authority of religious dogma and the old philosophic tradition, maintained the separation of values from the arts of life.

Dewey's analysis of the nature of the crisis in modern thought suggested the methods by which he proposed to deal with it. The conflict was clearly a struggle between science and religion, for every issue was necessarily resolved into a contest between the claims of the natural and the supernatural realms to furnish the sanction for values. Thus Dewey maintained the adequacy of a contingent justification for norms and ends and attacked any and every proposal to attach to values an absolute status or meaning. His solution for the problem may therefore be dealt with under two headings: (1) his rejection of the supernatural; an analysis of the origin of the distinction between supernatural and natural, and his argument against the validity of all absolutes in applying philosophy to life; (2) his acceptance of the natural as ade-

[12] John Dewey, *A Common Faith*, p. 32.
[13] *The Quest for Certainty*, p. 42.
[14] *Ibid.*, p. 95.

quate for the emergence of values, and his explanation of the way in which religious ideals find their origin and end wholly within the contingent world.

Dewey maintained that all that man has been accustomed to think of as supernatural can be explained in purely naturalistic terms, and that the distinction between the supernatural and the natural is entirely arbitrary and artificial. The separation begins with the distinction between things of common usage subject to everyday control and things of less frequent association not so easily amenable to human governance. The former are accepted on terms of easy familiarity, while the latter are elevated to a plane of superior status and regard.[15] Gradually, as degrees of value are discriminated among the objects of utility, those goods of higher value or infrequent experience are also located in the superior realm. Finally, ideal values which do not exist at all in experience in their perfection are held to have a real existence in a realm outside nature and beyond experience. Dewey holds that the hypostatization of value to a supernatural realm of being is accepted by men as a substitute for the practical activity necessary to give values an embodiment in the real world. For Dewey, this subtle change of the physical into the metaphysical represents a lack of moral faith, for in making it men renounce their obligation to work for the improvement of the conditions of their lives.[16] Modern liberal theology, Dewey believed, has made a considerable advance over the position which held all human relationships to be tainted with the corruption of human nature. The liberal theologians affirm that whatever is significant in human relationships partakes of the character of the supernatural realm but is still qualitatively distinct from it. They thus maintain the existence of two separate systems of values, mutually complementary and sustaining. But even this accord Dewey finds unsatisfactory, and he calls for the utter destruction of the supernatural realm by invasion from the dominion of nature. The articles of capitulation would then agree that

in fact the values prized in those religions that have ideal elements are idealizations of things characteristic of natural association, which have then been projected into a supernatural realm for safe-keeping and sanction.[17]

Dewey therefore argued for the rejection of all absolutes because of their origin in contingent necessities and contingent problems; " 'the modern spirit,' " he believed, "[is] something which puts away the supernaturalism

---

[15] *Ibid.*, p. 13.

[16] *A Common Faith*, pp. 21–22.

[17] *Ibid.*, p. 73.

of the race's immaturity . . ."[18] Supernaturalism was the product of man's primitive precariousness. When man found himself confronted in actual experience by values that were both unstable and dubious, he responded by projecting them, in a perfect or ideal form, into a realm of essence or a heaven beyond the earthly skies.[19] His repudiation of the Christian view of man as a finite creature Dewey shows most clearly in his belief that the methods of science will annul man's precariousness and remove him from the state of anxiety in which he sees his accomplishments and his prospects as subject to the ultimate determination of God.

Indeed, no problem causes Dewey greater difficulty than the problem of accounting for human evil. The tendency of religion to refer evil to the sinfulness of man, to the corruption of his heart, or to his self-love and love of power as causes seems to Dewey only another example of the way in which the attribution of values to the supernatural robs religious ideals of their power to transform the world. Such general moral causes he finds at the same intellectual level as the appeal to abstract powers or demons to explain the phenomena of physical science or the facts of bodily disease. They support the reign of mere accident as an explanation for the conduct of human affairs, and by stifling the growth of social intelligence they rob the individual of his responsibility for working improvement in human society.[20] Dewey sees the ascription of finitude to man merely as an effort to justify the avoidance of problems which invite man's participation on the assumption that he possesses sufficient power to effect significant changes in his life or in his environment. The distinction between finite and infinite, Dewey believes, is derived from that more fundamental separation of natural from supernatural, which reflects man's propensity to classify objects in terms of the ease or the difficulty with which he can control them.

The most widespread of these classificatory devices, the one of greatest popular appeal, is that which divides existence into the supernatural and the natural. Men may fear the gods but it is axiomatic that the gods have nothing to fear. They lead a life of untroubled serenity, the life that pleases them. There is a long story between the primitive forms of this division of objects of experience and the dialectical imputation to the divine of omnipotence, omniscience, eternity and infinity, in contrast with the attribution to man and experienced nature of finitude, weakness, limitation, struggle and change. But in the make-up of human psychology

---

[18] John Dewey, "Experience, Knowledge and Value: A Rejoinder," in Paul Arthur Schilpp (ed.), *The Philosophy of John Dewey* ("The Library of Living Philosophers," Vol. I [Evanston, 1939]), p. 596.

[19] *The Quest for Certainty*, pp. 33–34.

[20] *A Common Faith*, pp. 77–78.

the later history is implicit in the early crude division. One realm is the home of assured appropriation and possession; the other of striving, transiency and frustration. How many persons are there today who conceive that they have disposed of ignorance, struggle and disappointment by pointing to man's "finite" nature—as if finitude signifies anything else but an abstract classificatory naming of certain concrete and discriminable traits of nature itself—traits of nature which generate ignorance, arbitrary appearance and disappearance, failure and striving. It pleases man to substitute the dialectic exercise of showing how the "finite" can exist with or within the "infinite" for the problem of dealing with the contingent, thinking to solve the problem by distinguishing and naming its factors. Failure of the exercise is certain, but the failure can be flourished as one more proof of the finitude of man's intellect, and the needlessness because impotency of endeavor of "finite" creatures to attack ignorance and oppressive fatalities. Wisdom then consists in administration of the temporal, finite and human in its relation to the eternal and infinite, by means of dogma and cult, rather than in regulation of the events of life by understanding of actual conditions.[21]

It was clear to Dewey that the reference of natural social values by dialectic to antecedent absolute being instead of to consequent social action at the level of the contingent had resulted in their depreciation. But there were other pernicious consequences as well. It promoted a spirit of dogmatism and division.[22] It invited the exclusive attention to individual salvation which opened Christianity to the charge of concern for private interests. It supported a pessimistic outlook upon sin and social evil, but this in turn was capable of sudden transmutation into optimism when the establishment of a satisfactory relationship with the supernatural worked the miracle of regeneration in the human heart. And finally, it worked so little change in the actual conditions of the problem that it tended to support the conclusion that only supernatural aid could better them.[23] This was the impasse to which the "great separation" had brought the struggle for a better social order. To praise thinking above action because action is held to be suffused with evil is to help maintain the kind of world in which the arena for evil action is enlarged and extended.[24] But the rejection of absolutes did not mean to Dewey the abandonment of ideals. Instead it meant that values must be recaptured from the realm in which science could not reach them and returned to the contingent world. He called for the union of the ideal and the actual—not a mystical union, but a union which was properly described as natural and moral. And

[21] John Dewey, *Experience and Nature*, pp. 54–55.
[22] Dewey, in Schilpp, *The Philosophy of John Dewey*, p. 595.
[23] *A Common Faith*, pp. 46–47.
[24] *The Quest for Certainty*, p. 138.

this end was to be achieved through the methods of education and inquiry, for "Imagination of ideal ends pertinent to actual conditions represents the fruition of a disciplined mind."[25]

From his arguments against supernaturalism Dewey turns to a consideration of the religious possibilities of the world of natural contingencies. It is ideal, he maintains, for religion to advance pretentious claims for the absolute validity of its doctrinal pronouncements, for at every turn these can be shown to be embedded in the natural world. That religion should assert such ultimate claims is the more amazing in view of the fact that the religious groups have themselves been responsible for their continual involvement in the contingent world. Religion has committed itself, Dewey sees, to assertions about "astronomical, geological, biological subject-matter; about questions of anthropology, literary criticism, and history."[26] As science in these fields has advanced, religion has fought a losing battle and has been forced to retreat because it has assumed a rivalry with science about the structure of the natural world. Dewey rightly recognizes that in consequence of this conflict the Church has withdrawn into a position of isolation, into which it had been helped by its prideful pretension to an exclusive virtue and spirituality. Thus the Church pretends to be at once both within and without the world. From its defeats at the hands of science whenever it pushes its claims to absolute authority into the realm of the contingent, it withdraws into its historic isolation from the problems of society and advances the doctrine of dualism of nature and spirit as its justification. On the other side of ecclesiastical pretension to a privileged position in the pronouncement of value judgments is ecclesiastical condemnation to an inferior position of other associations which supply human needs. This attitude results in what Dewey holds to be the most serious of all the consequences of the hiatus between fact and value—the irresponsibility of individuals and groups stigmatized as "inferior" by the Church.[27] On the ecclesiastical side, meanwhile, the traditional emphasis of religion upon personal salvation has shifted the end of moral action from the benefits it should bring to the human community to the consequences for one's self. And when to all this is added the patent incapacity and failure of those professing religious principles to apply them constantly to the problems of criticism and judgment in the fields of morals, politics, and art, it becomes apparent to what an alarming extent the assertion of a privileged authority by the Church has issued in its abandonment of the arena of social action.[28]

---

[25] *A Common Faith*, p. 52.   [26] *The Quest for Certainty*, p. 303.
[27] *Ibid.*, p. 308.   [28] *Ibid.*, p. 70.

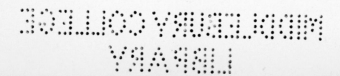

Principles that cannot be applied are no principles at all; thus the impoverishment of the modern religious liberal is the bankruptcy of his social theology. What is the answer? It is clear, for Dewey, that if a religion of the supernatural is not adequate to deal with the problems of the contingent world, one must turn to nature and experience for more adequate guidance.

The reconciliation of ideal values and practical affairs was to be found, Dewey thought, at the level of active participation in the problems of the contingent world. At the level of action, one necessarily and naturally employs the methods of science to assure a satisfactory outcome, and the distinction between thought and act, between what is theoretical and what is practical, disappears. The engineer, the physician, and the moralist all deal with subject matter which is practical because it concerns things to be done and how to do them. But they are all likewise concerned with theory, for they propose hypotheses by means of which to do their job and to test its adequacy when done. Like the philosopher, they commit themselves also to the canons of fairness, impartiality, internal consistency, and external evidence, seeking to purify their minds "as far as is humanly possible of bias and of that favoritism for one kind of conclusion rather than another which distorts observation and introduces an extraneous factor into reflection."[29] Philosophy, Dewey believes, cannot successfully maintain its claim to be an "intellectual" pursuit on any other basis—certainly not on the claim to deal with a subject matter fixed in antecedent reality. He calls upon philosophy to concern itself with proximate rather than ultimate problems, and he suggests that when once problems of the general welfare rather than those of narrow personal concern become the legitimate interest of philosophy, it will outgrow its tendency to disparage the practical.[30]

When this happens, said Dewey, philosophy will acknowledge the validity of the methods of science and make use of them. He insists that the mere employment of the skills and techniques of science will of itself destroy the status in antecedent being assigned to values. For the method of science is essentially a method of instituting deliberately and purposefully a definite and specified course of changes in the objects of experimentation. The other metaphysics, by contrast, specifies a changeless reality. Science changes reality itself as it employs its new and revolutionary method and ideal. "It is its glory, not its condemnation, that its subject-matter develops as the method is improved."[31] What happens, then, to the reality which is the subject matter

---

[29] Ibid., p. 68.
[30] Ibid., pp. 68–69.   [31] A Common Faith, p. 39.

of science is that it is removed once and for all and completely from the realm
of the absolute to that of the contingent. In Dewey's terms, this means that
the subject matter of science is transformed from objects to data. Objects are
absolutes; they are finalities, complete in themselves, calling only for definition, classification, and acceptance as unchangeable entities in the universe.
Data, on the other hand, are merely items of evidence; they are "given," so
that they may themselves be transformed by science into something more
adequate for human needs.[32] From this point of view it becomes immediately
clear that the methods of science are destructive of religion in the commonly
accepted sense—that is, as faith in, and worship of, a realm of being which
transcends the contingencies of time and nature. Indeed, Dewey holds that
the religious disposition had its origin in an atmosphere which enlisted and
regimented the resources of society in magic, divination, and "ritualistic ceremonies" precisely because men lacked the instruments and skills which science
later provided.[33] What Dewey defines as the religious disposition is, in fact,
the disposition to ascribe significance to the mere accidental character in
events—a disposition which of course runs counter to the quest of science for
relationships among the occurrences of the physical world. The only way in
which attainable possibilities may be projected and striven for in the real
world is by supplanting the religious disposition with an attitude congenial
to the methods of science.

There are positive, as well as negative, consequences to be expected from
the employment of the methods of science. Not only does science accomplish
the liquidation of values as absolute, but it guarantees their emergence from
the contingencies of life and action. All values which men are accustomed to
locate in the realm of the supernatural and dignify as religious Dewey finds
rooted in nature and in experience. This position Dewey maintained steadfastly following the publication of one of his earliest articles on the religious
problem in 1908. Religious values are rooted in democracy and science.[34]
They are a natural expression of human experience which emerges from
science as "undogmatic reverence for truth in whatever form it presents itself," and from democracy as "the moral significance of . . . a way of living
together."[35] The contingent world, "the community of causes and consequences," "the mysterious totality of being" is their matrix. From this source
the imagination projects them as "directive criteria and as shaping purposes."[36]

---

[32] *The Quest for Certainty*, p. 99.   [33] *Ibid.*, p. 10.
[34] John Dewey, "Religion and Our Schools," *Hibbert Journal*, July 1908, p. 799.
[35] Dewey in Schilpp, *The Philosophy of John Dewey*, p. 597.
[36] *A Common Faith*, p. 85.

When they break away from rites, symbols, and dogmas they attest an integrity of mind which is "potentially much more religious than all it is displacing."[37] At its highest level this integrity rises to a conception of "God" which for Dewey denotes certain portions of the world's life taken in its ideal aspects.[38] Dewey's conception of God is thus of the same order as that of the social evolutionists. As the ideal and purposive possibilities grasped by man for the reconstruction of his life and his environment it seems to liberate man from the determinisms of nature. But as the nexus of "all the natural forces and conditions—including man and human association" which contribute to the ideal and promote its growth—it is clear that this conception of God ends by destroying the freedom which it had seemed to promise.[39]

But if the texture of values that man uses to actualize the possibilities and potentialities of life is generated by forces in nature and society, it is unified and supported, solidified and made coherent, by the action that vitalizes ideals and puts them to work in the arena of concrete accomplishments. Thus Dewey's view of values is always of values at work; his attention fixes exclusively upon the changes being perpetually wrought in the universe; his philosophy is essentially a philosophy of action, so that the ideals which emerge from nature become real only to the extent that they are turned back into their source and leave it different from what it was before. The highest of all values is this "*active* relation between ideal and actual."[40] Man's chief concern is thus to make his values more secure in existence. From this point of view a truly religious attitude surrenders all beliefs whatsoever, even beliefs about values, and affirms only "the one value of discovering the possibilities of the actual and striving to realize them."[41] Here the emphasis rests almost wholly on the fact of activity, or activity accompanied by a sense of tension or impediment in the face of obstructions. But how to recognize such obstructions when they occur or to plot a course to avoid them is impossible if the only directive is to strive. An idealism of action such as Dewey describes looks only to the future, for its end and aim is not to know but to do. Indeed, knowing is defined as "a means of secular control,"[42] as a method of introducing changes to alter the course of future events, a definition which destroys the past as an object of knowledge because the past is not subject to the purposeful changes

[37] "Religion and Our Schools," *Hibbert Journal*, July 1908, p. 808.
[38] See Henry Nelson Wieman and Bernard Eugene Meland, *American Philosophies of Religion* (Chicago, 1936), p. 275.
[39] *A Common Faith*, p. 50.
[40] *Ibid.*, p. 51.
[41] *The Quest for Certainty*, p. 304.
[42] *Ibid.*, p. 100.

with which Dewey is concerned. The identification of knowing with doing thus requires the elimination of all religious implications from human activity because, as Dewey is aware throughout, religious values carry a warrant of allegiance to principle of which the contingencies of experience are necessarily ignorant. No knowledge can be demonstrated apart from activity. No activity is valid except activity that is associated with the changing texture of contingent relationships. No beliefs and judgments are meaningful apart from the consequences of action undertaken in their behalf. When these propositions associating thought and action are acknowledged, Dewey believed, then it will be recognized that "the problem of the intrinsic relation of science to value is wholly artificial."[43]

Since Dewey's analysis of the place of values in nature and experience rests upon the broad proposition that values are real only in so far as they are woven into the texture of life's ceaseless activity, it follows that his conclusions regarding the position of religion must emphasize the effects which may be attributed to the actual religious quality in experience. Hence for Dewey religion is predicative or adjectival rather than substantive. In *A Common Faith* he distinguishes between religion or religions and "the religious." Religions are bound by dogma, creed, and organization. They carry over from the past innumerable devices fashioned for contingent needs and relevant to a previous state of culture. "The religious," on the other hand, is a quality attaching to a person possessed by a faith in "inclusive ideal ends" which govern his desires and choices, thereby moving him constantly in the direction of unification of the self.[44] In the words of one of Dewey's interpreters, to be religious

is to give unqualified allegiance to an imaginative ideal, based on the heart's deepest desire, which directs our fundamental choices, and does not yield before the tyranny of force and chance.[45]

It is an objection to Dewey's view of "the religious" as the ideal dynamic of action that it does not adequately discriminate among ideals. The self may achieve sufficient unification to participate in the social struggle without thereby rising to a level of moral insight adequate for the constant evaluation and criticism of its own actions and allegiances. Faith in the validity of the consequences of action is no more a guaranty of value than faith in the validity of a religious formula or symbol. Nor does it suffice to locate "the religious"

[43] *The Quest for Certainty*, p. 43.
[44] *A Common Faith*, p. 33.
[45] Sidney Hook, *John Dewey: An Intellectual Portrait* (New York, 1939), p. 219.

indifferently in all types of activity and endeavor. Dewey holds that there is a "religious" quality in the scientist's faith in the continued disclosing of truth, or that "religious" commitments are involved in art, political life, or even business if in making them we risk our lives as a pledge to fulfill our commitment. But this explanation still leaves the question of just what the nature of the "religious" commitment in science, art, or politics really is. At most, Dewey's "faith" seems to denote a rather naïve confidence in human intelligence, aided by the mysterious operations of nature, to work its way out of any predicament in which it may find itself:

. . . faith in the possibilities of continued and rigorous inquiry . . . trusts that the natural interactions between man and his environment will breed more intelligence and generate more knowledge provided the scientific methods that define intelligence in operation are pushed further into the mysteries of the world, being themselves promoted and improved in the operation. There is such a thing as faith in intelligence becoming religious in quality . . .[46]

Dewey thus inverts the orthodox Augustinian relationship between faith and knowledge. Whereas the Christian tradition makes the highest degree of self-transcendence a prerequisite of knowledge, Dewey proposes instead that the working of human intelligence will generate all that can be denoted as essentially "religious" in life.

Dewey's definition of religious faith notices two elements by means of which its working may be identified in human personality. One is the integration of self through the operation of experiences which bring a "better, deeper and enduring adjustment" in life. Dewey holds that such experiences, occurring much more frequently than is commonly supposed, spring from "conditions of nature and human association" and are incorrectly associated with the idea of invisible powers simply because the adjustment which characterizes them proceeds from sources beyond conscious deliberation and purpose.[47] Such an adjustment carries with it a "reconciliation" and a "sense of security and stability." This function of "the religious" contradicts the Christian insight into man's uneasy conscience which transcends his capacity for righteous action and will give him no security while life lasts. But for Dewey, "Peace in action not after it is the contribution of the ideal to conduct."[48]

The other element which helps Dewey to recognize the "religious" quality in man is man's capacity for placing himself in a context beyond him-

[46] *A Common Faith*, p. 26.

[47] *Ibid.*, p. 14.

[48] Edward L. Schaub, "Dewey's Interpretation of Religion," in Schilpp, *The Philosophy of John Dewey*, p. 398; Dewey, *Human Nature and Conduct* (New York, 1922), p. 264.

self. Thus Dewey recognizes that it is a characteristic of the religious experience "to sustain and expand" us in feebleness and failure "by the sense of an enveloping whole." To place one's self in context is to introduce perspective, and for Dewey "whatever introduces genuine perspective is religious."[49] Man in isolation from the world of physical nature and his fellows is "essentially unreligious,"[50] whereas the self which achieves its unification through integration into "that imaginative totality we call the Universe"[51] is dignified and ennobled. Religion liberates us from the conceit of carrying the load of the universe, and when we capture the "sense of the whole" that lives amid our flickering, inconsequential acts, "we put off mortality and live in the universal."[52] Dewey's credo is perhaps no better formulated than in a passage at the end of *Experience and Nature* in which he emphasizes once again the source of power which springs from man's intellect and from his involvement in the universe.

When we have used our thought to its utmost and have thrown into the moving unbalanced balance of things our puny strength, we know that though the universe slay us still we may trust, for our lot is one with whatever is good in existence. We know that such thought and effort is one condition of the coming into existence of the better. As far as we are concerned it is the only condition, for it alone is in our power. To ask more than this is childish; but to ask less is a recreance no less egotistic, involving no less a cutting of ourselves from the universe than does the expectation that it meet and satisfy our every wish. To ask in good faith as much as this from ourselves is to stir into motion every capacity of imagination, and to exact from action every skill and bravery.[53]

It is significant that Dewey's essential affirmation is that man is a part of universal goodness, for, like all the proponents of "natural religion," he could find no adequate explanation for the fact of evil.

In the course of this analysis of John Dewey's discussion of the relationship between science and religion several suggestions have been made in criticism of his position from the standpoint of Christian presuppositions or on the assumption that there is meaning in the religious experience which a naturalistic philosophy does not adequately reveal. In the remaining paragraphs these criticisms will be summarized in order to clarify the bearing upon the basic religious issues of Dewey's treatment of the problem of science and religion.

The essential point around which this criticism turns is that Dewey's

---

[49] *A Common Faith*, p. 24.   [50] *Ibid.*, p. 25.   [51] *Ibid.*, p. 19.
[52] *Human Nature and Conduct*, p. 331.
[53] *Experience and Nature*, pp. 420–21.

discussion, in which the methods of science are properly uppermost, relates only to the contingent world, the only world to which the methods of science meaningfully apply. A philosophy of contingencies cannot comprehend phenomena which transcend contingent relationships, phenomena which, in other words, are religious. It follows, therefore, that when Dewey recasts all supernatural events in terms of nature he is surrendering for his analysis any claim to a hearing as a "religious" philosophy. Even as a philosophy of nature Dewey's treatment is open to serious objection. In spite of his effort to invert the relationship of knowledge theory and nature theory, Dewey ends by identifying knowing and doing, with the result that his system reduces to a highly complex and intricate epistemology.

Dewey's exclusive preoccupation with the contingent is apparent in every aspect of his treatment of the problem of the relationship of science and religion. His predilection for the methods of science as the only "practical" pattern for experience leads him to limit the sphere of what he calls "the religious" to the narrowest social limits. Human integrity narrowly considered as the unification of the self for active participation in the flux of life scarcely does justice to the soul that finds the center of its being at a level from which its own involvement in life is subject to criticism and amendment. Likewise, the most "universal" contingent context for human life comprehended in Dewey's analysis still falls far short of the fullness which attaches to membership in God. The only problems which have meaning for Dewey are those which could be solved by social adjustment. But the most profound of the genuinely religious problems, those which arise in moments of tragedy or in ages of widespread social catastrophe, are not touched by the ministrations of the social gospel.

Similarly, Dewey's concentration upon contingent problems blinds him to the completeness of man's dependence on nature and, conversely, to the extent of his freedom from its determinisms. Man's dependence upon nature is really much more profound than the proximate dependence upon environment which Dewey describes. Man's dependence is absolute, for man not only succumbs to death but knows that he will die. This is an awareness which itself transcends nature and points to an adjustment within the province of religion which constitutes man's freedom. Dewey's naturalism therefore does not do justice either to the profundity of man's natural dimension, which decrees death, or to his spiritual dimension, which annuls it.[54] Instead of

[54] Edward L. Schaub, "Dewey's Interpretation of Religion," in Schilpp, *The Philosophy of John Dewey*, pp. 415–16.

recognizing man's partiality and precariousness as a creature embedded in nature and looking to man's spiritual dimension as a source of his freedom within the limits of his finiteness, Dewey proposes to overcome man's natural anxiety and promises peace, security, and stability through co-operation with nature. From the standpoint of Christian theology this is not only an absurd pretension to power not within man's competence, but also an impious affront to God.

Perhaps the most glaring consequence of Dewey's concentration upon merely contingent problems is his utter powerlessness before the fact of evil. The existence of evil is a phenomenon too profound and recalcitrant to find an easy place in a scheme which is primarily concerned with comparing the anticipated and the actual consequences of a course of action. Christian insights locate evil in the nature of the anticipated consequences themselves, prior to and apart from the act, but Dewey destroys the distinction between purpose and act, and with this destruction he surrenders opportunity to pass judgment upon and assess responsibility for the consequences of an evil will.

It is consonant with Dewey's lack of an adequate treatment of the problem of evil that he has no sense of history. A concern for judgment upon human evil requires attention to history, for all moral judgments are historical judgments. Dewey, however, is concerned exclusively with the future, for it is only by reference to future consequences that his propositions can be said to be true or his ideals to have value. It goes without saying that a preoccupation with the future as the means of social action robs his proposals of adequate historical perspective. Most important from the Christian standpoint, Dewey's lack of history limits the validity of his judgments to a time span so short that, just as he fails to grasp their relationship to the pattern of human historic development, so also, and more tragically, he fails to appreciate the perspective beyond history from which alone the historical dimension becomes fully meaningful. The timelessness of Dewey's analysis is a characteristic product of the scientific attitude, whereas the historical relationships which he undervalues find their meaning through the religious insights denied by his contingent presuppositions.

A final criticism may be brought against the religious validity of Dewey's position in grounding his philosophy in the presuppositions of science and of democracy. The methods of science are by themselves inadequate as a source of values because they give no clue to the use which the products of science may be made to serve. Sheer intellectual inquiry is meaningless save on the assumption that it is inquiry into the nature of God's created world, and that by pushing inquiry forward man will come to love God as he learns to know his work. So also with democracy. The common life does not itself produce values; it serves values already given. Democracy is not an end in itself; its validity and its eternal power lie in the fact that it is the form of society best able to serve the highest possible end, and, conversely, that it is with the greatest difficulty corrupted and perverted to partial ends. The common life assumes the religious sense—what John Oman calls the sense of the sacred— as its ground, not as its result. Oman's position may be taken as an answer to Dewey in its emphasis upon the independence of the idea of absolute value.

And the question is [Oman writes] how such an illusion could arise out of mere mass feeling, and still more, how it could later develop into the only sanction which could be set up effectively against the mass mind. If the sense of the sacred were already there, it would naturally attach itself to the society in which we live and by which we live; but how, out of mere social, variable, and comparative values, could the idea of an absolute value, in the might of which man can stand alone over against his whole society, ever arise? Nothing is more certain than that the sacred claims to have its sanction in itself and to be corrupted when it is accepted as submission to public opinion.[55]

The common life is good for Christians not because it yields religious senti-ments and religious values but because it is the way to know Christ, in whose body all are members and in whose love all achieve their full stature.

Dewey's position on the relationship of science and religion is not that of the humanist who adopts the ethical principles of Christianity but denies that they imply a Christian metaphysics. Dewey denies Christian doctrine pri-marily because his system inevitably turns in upon itself by making the action of the individual its own norm and end. He denies essential religious prin-ciples because he withdraws from the only realm in which phenomena are truly religious, the realm of the supernatural. His solution, therefore, to the problem of the proper relationship of science and religion is the utter destruc-tion of religion.

[55] John W. Oman, "The Sphere of Religion," in Joseph Needham (ed.), *Science, Religion, and Reality* (New York, 1925), p. 279.

7

Fundamentalism Versus Modernism, 1920-30

THE DECADE of the 1920's witnessed a resurgence of the warfare between science and religion. It had its origin, in part at least, in the worship of science following the first World War. It reached its dramatic climax in the trial of John Thomas Scopes at Dayton, Tennessee, where the claims of science over scriptural inerrancy appeared to have won a resounding victory. After the Scopes trial the warfare was mitigated somewhat as liberal theologians offered easy explanations for the accommodation of religion and science. And at length, with the economic collapse of 1929, the conflict subsided as it became evident that social and economic problems had become for the moment more compelling for most Americans than were those of Biblical interpretation. In the interval, however, much had been said and written on both sides of the questions in dispute.

Although the conflict between religion and science has its roots deep in human nature—where man's quest for certitude and security encounters his acknowledgment that the proofs of the one and the guaranties of the other are never adequate—its manifestation in a particular period and area necessarily reflects the peculiar conditions of its setting. The United States in the 1920's, and particularly the Mississippi Valley, provided conditions which helped to make this phase of the conflict understandable. The struggle of the 'twenties was not grounded in a revival of historical studies as in the late nineteenth century, nor in the interest in human personality which illuminated the controversy centered in William James's *Varieties of Religious Experience* in the early twentieth. The controversy between the "fundamentalists" and "modernists," as the antagonists in the current battle came to be known, was occupied primarily with the moral issue. The main concern was whether the Bible, if challenged in its historical and scientific pronouncements, could still maintain the validity and power of its moral prescriptions; whether the scientist, no longer guided by Biblical commitments, could find in his purely intellectual presuppositions sufficient warrant for the moral life. The issue was not, as an English writer mistakenly assumed, "the credibility of the whole of Judges and the edibility of the whole of Jonah,"[1] but rather as Bryan saw it,

---

[1] Quoted in Howard Chandler Robbins, "Fundamentalism and Modernism," *The Forum*, May 1924, p. 652. According to this unfriendly critic, fundamentalism was the position "whose

a battle of the hosts of the Lord in a final grapple with the forces of Hell. The real point in dispute was whether the attack on the literal interpretation of the Old Testament might not also undermine the moral teaching of the New Testament. What the fundamentalist feared most was that the current criticism would weaken men not so much in manipulating logic and evidence as in struggling for righteousness in life. The warfare of the 'twenties was not a fight for obscurantism—it was, in the eyes of the fundamentalists, a crusade in the prophetic tradition against the forces of evil.

From this basic distinction between fundamentalist and modernist there followed important consequences. The fundamentalist, being already persuaded that he had the truth, believed that the moral problem was the central problem and, hence, that the meaning of life was to be found in the relationship of a god of righteousness to a man of sin. "The two great historic presuppositions, in the Fundamentalist view," one of its spokesmen held, "are God enveloped in a terrible righteousness, man as offending against His law and under His just wrath."[2] For the modernists, on the contrary, the dominant concern was the quest for truth. The defense of the modernist position in the current periodicals turned primarily on its effort to accommodate its dogma to the affirmations of science, a characteristic which Reinhold Niebuhr, writing at the end of the period, recognized as a fatal weakness. "The curse of modern religion," he observed, "is that it is so busy adjusting itself to the modern mind that it can find no energy to challenge the modern conscience."[3] The critics of modernism held that its preoccupation with intellectual considerations robbed it of moral fervor and initiative.

The fundamentalist-modernist controversy showed, in addition, a significant cleavage on social and economic issues. Areas of fundamentalist strength in the Mississippi Valley were the small towns and the rural sections, while the larger city churches found the modernist doctrines of the benevolence of God and the sinlessness of man congenial to the growing wealth and prosperity of the postwar years. Both houses identified their opponents with ideas or movements hostile to essential Americanism. For the modernist, the funda-

religious beliefs, whether they are true or whether they are not true, are based on the dogma of the verbal inerrancy of the Bible" (*Ibid.*, p. 651).

[2] J. Gresham Machen, "What Fundamentalism Stands for Now," quoted from the *New York Times* in *The Literary Digest*, July 11, 1925, p. 32. Another formulation of the issue was that proposed by the modernist Henry P. Van Dusen, who held that "humanism" confronted Barthian theology, Anglo-Catholicism, and Buchmanism. See "The Sickness of Liberal Religion," *The World Tomorrow*, August 1931, pp. 256–57.

[3] Reinhold Niebuhr, "Would Jesus be a Modernist Today?" *The World Tomorrow*, March 1929, p. 123.

mentalist was likely to be not only an opponent of evolution but also a sup-
porter or member of the Ku Klux Klan, a prohibitionist, a "snooper" or
regulator of private morals, an isolationist, and a proponent of state owner-
ship.[4] The fundamentalist, on the other hand, was equally confident that the
enemies of the commonwealth were universally enlisted in the rival camp.
"There is not a stranger combination in the world," observed a writer in the
publication, *Christian Fundamentals*, "than the one evolution produced. It
brings together the Reds of Russia, the university professors of Germany, England and America, the I.W.W.'s and every bum from the down-and-out
sections in every city in America. There are two classes of people that vote
together every time this subject is discussed, and that is the university crowd
and the social Reds, and they are practically alone in their advocacy of evolution."[5] An observer in the English *Contemporary Review* with more in-
genuity than insight associated fundamentalist theology in the Middle West
with the support of conservative economic presuppositions. The American
business world was fundamentalist, he believed, because of an "instinctive
recognition" that an attack on the established economic order would follow
quickly upon a challenge to traditional theology.[6] This, however, was the
view of one far off from the struggle. Actually, the class affiliations of the
fundamentalists of the Mississippi Valley were rather with the lower-middle-
class and farming elements than with the prosperous business and financial
classes whose contributions built the substantial metropolitan churches. And
the significant social and economic outcome of the controversy at the end of
the decade was the discovery that the fundamental doctrines were applicable
to social justice as well as to individual morality.

Granted that the fundamentalist and the modernist of the Middle West
dealt with different issues and relied upon different basic assumptions, yet
how far did these differences really separate them in their common membership in the Christian commonwealth? Some examples of the religious
thought of the period from both camps will facilitate appraisal. Prominent
at different levels of insight among the fundamentalists were William Jen-

[4] Rollin Lynde Hartt, "The Disruption of Protestantism," in *The Forum*, November 1925,
pp. 679–87. According to the historian Samuel Eliot Morison, Tennessee had been a "backwater,
untouched by any of the main currents of American life since 1865," and therefore it was not
surprising that modern scientific and social thought had not penetrated to its "cultural depths"
(*The Observer*, July 19, 1925).

[5] Harbor Allen, "The Anti-Evolution Campaign in America," *Current History*, September
1926, p. 897, quoting from *Christian Fundamentals*.

[6] S. K. Ratcliffe, "America and Fundamentalism," *Contemporary Review*, September 1925,
p. 289.

nings Bryan, active as orator and publicist until his death during the Scopes trial at Dayton in 1925, and Dr. William B. Riley of Minneapolis, one of the founders of the World's Christian Fundamentals Association, and a leading evangelist in the Valley during the decade.

No American was more prominently associated with the warfare of science and religion than the Great Commoner, whose career, identified throughout with the powers and limitations of the Middle West, came to an end after what he described as "the day I have waited for," the opportunity to do battle against the detractors of man's divine nature. Bryan had himself formulated the issues in his writings and speeches early in the decade. In "God and Evolution," published in the *New York Times* in February 1922, and in subsequent articles in the magazine, *The Forum*, he stated the case against Darwinism; and in his James Sprunt Lectures, under the title "In His Image" at the Union Theological Seminary in Virginia in 1922, he elaborated the theological considerations on which his opposition to the evolutionary doctrine was based.[7] Bryan's central proposition was that the Darwinian hypothesis was a menace to fundamental morality because by linking man with brute nature it obscured God and "weakened the virtues that rest upon the religious tie between God and man." Bryan endorsed the findings of the English sociologist Benjamin Kidd, whose *Science of Power*, published in 1918, had associated Darwinian and Nietzschean doctrines with the aggressive military policy of Imperial Germany. Darwinism, said Bryan, did more than destroy the faith of Christians; in addition, it was the basis for the class struggle in that it released the brute in man and intensified his awareness of class antagonisms. Finally, Darwinism discouraged efforts to alleviate social distress and instigate reforms because it held that natural selection precluded the possibility of human tampering with the historical process. Yet in his own appraisal of human nature Bryan abandoned the fundamentalists' profound insight into man's propensity to sin and placed himself alongside the modernist in his optimistic view of man's capacities for personal and social regeneration. Taking as his basic tenet the proposition that God had created man in his own image, Bryan charged his hearers to have faith—first, "in yourselves," second, "in mankind," third, "in your form of government," and fourth, "in God."[8] God came in a poor fourth in Bryan's enumeration, but faith in God he believed adequate, nevertheless, to guarantee the triumph of right. Thus Bryan shared the optimism of the modernists, their overestima-

[7] William Jennings Bryan, *In His Image* (New York, 1922).
[8] *Ibid.*, pp. 259–65.

tion of man's capacity to find solutions for his problems, their blindness to his essential limitations amid the problems of the postwar decade.

While Bryan from the platform and with the pen provided the prominence of national leadership for fundamentalism, a legion of lesser men were the shock troops who bore the brunt of the battle. Chief among them was Riley, whose many publications, bearing such titles as *The Crisis of the Church, The Menace of Modernism,* and *Inspiration or Evolution,* furnished the systematic body of ideas from which the fundamentalists drew freely. Riley held Darwinism responsible for the war of 1914, and believed that "the recent baptism of blood . . . as compared with the baptism yet to come, [was] as a local shower to the flood that will prevail over every mountain." The Darwinian doctrine, said Riley, was responsible for the social anarchy of the postwar years. The doctrine of kinship with the ape robbed man of his essential dignity, and responsibility for preaching it rested heavily upon those "capped and gowned men, drawing salaries from tax payers or benevolently inclined persons," who were seducing people from essential Christian tenets to the philosophies of Hegel, Marx, and Darwin. The fundamentalists occupied an anti-intellectualist position, but they were aware of a deep source of strength in the grass roots of popular approval. What they objected to most was the fact that the modernists were merely teaching philosophy, not preaching religion. Their quarrel with the God of the liberals was that He lacked the common touch. "The God of a Coe, a Rauschenbusch, a Frank Crane," said Riley, "has played the aristocrat long enough and must now descend to his proper place 'in a democracy.' " The fundamentalist was in the tradition of Middle Western democracy in his appeal to the ultimate judgment of the people. And he found theological justification for his democracy in the doctrine that man was created in God's image, not evolved from lower forms of life.[9]

The spokesmen of religion and science alike recognized the challenge of Middle Western fundamentalism to the naturalistic and aristocratic implications of the doctrine of evolution. Harry Emerson Fosdick, throughout the decade the leader of modernist thought from his pulpit on Riverside Drive, undertook again and again to answer the charges of the fundamentalists. He recognized the force of their claim that Darwinism did injustice to the dignity of man. "If evolution does thus brutalize man's conception of his own nature," he wrote, "it is a public enemy." But Fosdick denied that the Darwinian hypothesis necessarily degraded man, and pointed, instead, to

[9] W. B. Riley, *Inspiration or Evolution* (Cleveland, 1926), pp. 44, 45, 62.

the fallacy of evaluating anything in terms of its origins. He would reverse the process: "Everything is to be judged," he insisted, "by what it has capacity to become." Thus in the evolution of the race, as in the growth of the human individual, the soul at last emerges like a temple from the scaffolding within which it was built. "No matter by what route he came," Fosdick concluded, "man is what he is, with his intelligence, his moral life, his spiritual possibilities, his capacity for fellowship with God."[10]

Professional scientists, by virtue of their special concern being with knowledge instead of morals, were naturally more at home with the modernist view. And the response of the scientists to the fundamentalist challenge was even more positive than that of the modernists themselves. From his laboratory at Columbia University and his office at the American Museum of Natural History, Henry Fairfield Osborn quickly entered the lists against Bryan. Osborn answered Bryan's articles "God and Evolution" and "Mr. Bryan Speaks to Darwin" with rejoinders entitled "Evolution and Religion" and "The Earth Speaks to Bryan." In the former he affirmed that evolution was "the most firmly established truth in the natural universe." In the latter he marshaled the evidence in favor of evolution, including the recent discovery in Bryan's native Nebraska of a diminutive tooth which Osborn acclaimed "the herald of our knowledge of anthropoid apes in America." The moral problem, about which the fundamentalists had had much to say, Osborn reduced to the fairly simple query, "Are we living in such a way as to have descendants?" and he expressed the hope that "Nature" and religion would so govern the conduct of America's young men and women as to enable them to evolve in the right direction![11]

In the more technical language of the professional philosopher, Alfred North Whitehead appealed in his *Science and the Modern World* for increasing accuracy in religious expression disengaged from religious imagery, and in his Lowell Lectures for 1926, *Religion in the Making*, for a more adequate metaphysical basis for theology.[12] The physical scientists, to whom Whitehead assigned the second task, undertook to accomplish it by affirming that adequate religious notions could rest on fundamental natural laws demonstrable by science. The astronomer Henry Norris Russell, for example, in

[10] Harry Emerson Fosdick, *Adventurous Religion and Other Essays* (New York, 1926), pp. 128, 131.

[11] Henry Fairfield Osborn, *Evolution and Religion in Education: Polemics of the Fundamentalist Controversy of 1922 to 1926* (New York, 1926).

[12] Alfred North Whitehead, *Science and the Modern World* (New York, 1925), chap. xii, *passim.*, and *Religion in the Making* (New York, 1926), pp. 85–86.

his Terry Lectures of 1925, asserted that the evolutionary struggle belonged
to the surface of things, whereas the invariant law underneath it affirmed an
order and harmony in nature, and a Power behind it.[13] And so also the
physicist Robert A. Millikan, who argued in the same lectureship three years
later that religion itself proved the fact of evolution in the history of its own
development from crude beginnings to its present state.[14] But upon the issues
which were central for the fundamentalists—namely, man's moral nature and
and his power through the operation of the democratic process to control
teachings which might corrupt it—the philosopher and scientist raised no
loud clamor.

Upon the Mississippi Valley the impact of the controversy between fundamentalism and modernism in the decade of the 'twenties was most notable
in the area of education, as evidenced in attempts by the states to prohibit or
control the teaching of evolution. Not only in Tennessee was the teaching
of man's kinship with the lower forms of life attacked as contrary to public
policy. An antievolution law failed by only twenty votes in the Missouri
Legislature, and in Arkansas and in Kentucky by only a single vote.[15] In
the Upper Valley, modernist clergymen and educators touched with Darwinism were singled out for censure by the fundamentalists. Not even liberal
Wisconsin escaped. In 1925 the pastor of Christ Presbyterian Church in
Madison was accused of heresy and evolutionism before the Synod, and when
he was acquitted his case was carried before the General Assembly of the
Church. At the University of Wisconsin, Professor E. A. Ross was a favorite
subject for attack. When Bryan heard that a professor at the University of
Wisconsin was telling his class that the Bible was a collection of myths he
brought the matter to the attention of President Birge. The president "criti-
cized me," Bryan wrote, "but avoided all reference to the professor."[16] Similar
instances could be multiplied almost at will.

The major result of the controversy, however, was not merely to discredit
Bryan and the fundamentalists. To be sure, Bryan's leadership of the warfare
against Darwinism made him the target for much unfair criticism. It was
probably not true, as David Starr Jordan observed in letters to a friend, that
Bryan had "never read a bound book," that "he has only emotional attitudes
toward what he never tried to understand," that he "is not the opposite of

[13] Henry Norris Russell, *Fate and Freedom*, p. 79.
[14] Robert Andrews Millikan, *Evolution in Science and Religion* (New Haven, 1928), pp.
65–66.
[15] For a summary of state laws against the teaching of evolution in the schools see Maynard
Shipley, *The War on Modern Science* (New York, 1927).
[16] Bryan, *op. cit.*, p. 120.

science, but represents the backwash of knowledge."[17] Unfortunately the controversy often centered upon the question of the literal versus the figurative interpretation of the Scriptures, which was really secondary, rather than upon the question of the nature of man, which was central. For whereas the fundamentalist and the modernist disputed the meaning and scope of scriptural statements and their relationship to the findings of science, they agreed about man's essential nature and destiny, his natural goodness and bright prospects for the future. Whether God had created man complete and perfect from the primordial clay or inherent and potential in the evolutionary process mattered little, so long as both parties looked eagerly and confidently upon man's power to achieve the good life for himself and the good society for his fellows. The fundamentalist and the modernist shared an optimistic view of man which indeed seemed entirely justified by the prosperity of the postwar boom of the 'twenties. But throughout the controversy the modernist emphasized the redeeming power of the enlightened mind while the fundamentalist endorsed the untutored religious insights of the common man. Thus every religious denomination was set to thinking about doctrinal questions.[18]

The current interest in theology owes no small debt to the religious controversy of the 'twenties, in which both antagonists acknowledged the relevance of theological issues. Against the modernist plea for an open mind the fundamentalist answered in the words of Walter Lippmann, whose University of Virginia Lectures of 1928, *American Inquisitors*, expressed the essential ambiguity which the controversy involved. "For you," said Lippmann's fundamentalist to the modernists, "there is nothing at stake but a few tentative opinions . . . [You ask] that I submit the foundation of my life to the destructive effects of your skepticism, your indifference, and your good nature. You ask me to smile and to commit suicide . . ."[19] But the fundamentalist did not smile, and certainly he did not commit suicide. Instead, as the 'twenties ended, he joined forces with the modernist for the time being in extolling the divinity of man and awaited a more favorable time to argue the relevance of fundamental doctrines. The writings of many contemporary theologians suggest that this time is now at hand.

[17] Jordan to Scudder Klyce, October 23, November 15, December 10, 1923, Jordan Correspondence, Vol. LXXXIII.

[18] Curtis Lee Laws, in *The Watchman-Examiner*. Quoted in "What Fundamentalism Has Achieved," *The Literary Digest*, February 4, 1928, p. 32.

[19] Walter Lippmann, *American Inquisitors* (New York, 1928), pp. 65–66.